UP POMPEII

by Miles Tredinnick

Based on the characters created by
Talbot Rothwell and Sid Colin

JOSEF WEINBERGER PLAYS

LONDON

Up Pompeii

First published in 2012
by Josef Weinberger Ltd
12-14 Mortimer Street, London W1T 3JJ
www.josef-weinberger.com / plays@jwmail.co.uk

ISBN: 978 0 85676 338 0

UP POMPEII

Up Pompeii was first presented by Bruce James Productions at the Pomegranate Theatre, Chesterfield on January 25th 2011 before a national UK tour. The cast in order of appearance was as follows:

CORNEOUS	Ben Roddy
AMMONIA	Jacqueline Roberts
LUDICRUS SEXTUS	Richard Colson
EROTICA	Cloudia Knight
LURCIO	Damian Williams
SENNA THE SOOTHSAYER	Sophie Leigh
VOLUPTUA	Mieke Dockley
CAPTAIN TREACHERUS	Andrew Ryan
KRETINUS	Neil Bull
NAUSIUS	Alex Newbold
SUSPENDA	Lucinda Kennard

Directed by Bruce James
Designed by Charles Camm
Lighting by Geoff Gilder

Cast in order of appearance:

Corneous (a footman)
Ammonia (the Mistress)
Ludicrus Sextus (the Master)
Erotica (Ludicrus & Ammonia's daughter)
Lurcio (a slave)
Senna the Soothsayer
Voluptua (a slave girl)
Captain Treacherus (a slave trader)
Kretinus (Treacherus's sidekick)
Nausius (Ludicrus & Ammonia's son)
Suspenda (the well known nymphomaniac & beauty)

The action of the play takes place in the courtyard of Ludicrus Sextus's villa in Pompeii.

Act One

Mid-morning on a summer's day

Act Two

Later the same day. The action is continuous.

Time: Ancient Pompeii.

ACT ONE.

As the audience are taking their seats before the curtain goes up, SENNA *the old hag soothsayer should walk up and down the aisles crying out "Woe, woe and thrice woe" and generally giving us the benefit of her nightly visitations. Maybe she could offer members of the audience a prediction or two?*

The courtyard garden of LUDICRUS SEXTUS'S *opulent villa. Stage right, we can see entrances leading off to a bedroom and also into the house. There are also some steps leading up to a bathroom, centre. Beside the steps is a small walk-in cupboard.*

UL is a large iron gate and various pillars surrounding the garden. There is also a water well with a sitting stone in front of it where LURCIO *will attempt to deliver his "Prologue".*

DL is a double-doors entrance to the household stable. The doors are open and we can see a cart inside.

When the curtain rises the stage is empty but the voices of LUDICRUS SEXTUS *and his wife* AMMONIA *can be clearly heard coming from inside the house. They are having a big row!*

LUDICRUS	(*off*) I'm sorry my dear but I distinctly remember telling you.
AMMONIA	(*off*) You did not! I distinctly remember that you did not tell me.
LUDICRUS	(*off*) Well I'm telling you now.
AMMONIA	(*off*) It's no good now is it? What's the point in telling me now?
	(CORNEOUS, *the footman, comes out of the house carrying two bags. He is quite*

*oblivious to his Master and Mistress's
argument. He stands in front of the sitting
stone and takes careful aim before throwing
one of the bags into the cart. It lands
directly in the cart. He then repeats this
with the second bag but this time, as a
challenge to himself, faces away from the
cart and throws the bag behind him over his
head. Again it's a direct hit landing in the
cart. He turns to face the audience with a
satisfied smile on his face and takes a bow
and, hopefully, applause. He then returns
into the house.*)

AMMONIA   (*off*) You're so thoughtless Ludicrus.

LUDICRUS   (*off*) The trouble with you my dear is that
               you don't listen.

               (AMMONIA *enters from inside the house. She
               is fuming with anger.*)

AMMONIA   How can I listen when you won't tell me
               anything?

               (LUDICRUS SEXTUS *follows her out.*)

LUDICRUS   I told you last week. I have to go to Rome
               for the weekend. It's very important.

AMMONIA   What's so important about Rome?

LUDICRUS   I have to present a new bill to the Senate.

AMMONIA   You're always presenting new bills to the
               Senate.

LUDICRUS   Well I am a Senator dear. It's my job. (*He
               sits down on the stone.*)

AMMONIA   But why this weekend? The height of the
               social calendar. We should be making
               friends and losing money at the chariot
               races, not sitting in the dull old Senate. (*She
               sits down beside him.*)

LUDICRUS   My new bill is very important.

AMMONIA   More important than your wife's happiness?

LUDICRUS   Of course not. It's just a question of
               priorities.

               (*Their pretty late-teenage daughter* EROTICA
               *comes out of the house. She is totally
               preoccupied with writing a chalk message
               onto a slate.*)

AMMONIA   So why is this bill so important?

LUDICRUS   It is my anti-vice bill. There's far too much
               sex going on and I'm not having any of it.

AMMONIA   (*sotto*) That makes two of us then.

LUDICRUS   The whole of the Empire has gone sex mad!

AMMONIA   Not round here it hasn't.

LUDICRUS   It needs clearing up. Nowadays people are
               too decadent, too promiscuous. We're living
               in a permissive society Ammonia.

EROTICA   Daddy, how do you spell "fancy"?

LUDICRUS   (*ignores* EROTICA) There's a strong swing
               in the Senate towards tougher action. The
               atmosphere is right for a new bill to be
               introduced. This could do me a lot of good
               my dear.

AMMONIA	In what way?
LUDICRUS	Well . . . How does the title "Empress" grab you?
AMMONIA	I don't think it would suit you. You haven't got the legs.
LUDICRUS	Not for me, for you! I've got ambitions Ammonia. I intend to reach the top. This bill will be a necessary stepping stone.
EROTICA	Are there two 'e's in "meeting"?
AMMONIA	Well . . . I just wish you'd given me some warning Ludicrus. (*She throws her arms up in despair.*) I don't even know what they're wearing in Rome this year.
LUDICRUS	But . . . but you're not coming with me my dear.
AMMONIA	(*standing up*) Why ever not? It's a wife's place to be by her husband's side when he tells everyone to stop enjoying themselves.
EROTICA	How do you spell "desire"?
LUDICRUS	No, Ammonia. It would be far too boring for you. Hanging around Rome whilst we make all our dreary speeches.
AMMONIA	Oh I'm sure I could find something to do. Hunt for bargains in the markets or go to the Coliseum. I've heard that the gladiators are more handsome and stronger than ever this year.
LUDICRUS	(*standing up*) I will not hear of it my dear. You and Erotica must go and spend the

weekend with my mother at Tedius in the countryside.

AMMONIA   (*horrified*) With Botoxia? In the sticks?

LUDICRUS   I've made all the arrangements.

AMMONIA   But Ludicrus . . .

LUDICRUS   No arguments. You're sure to have a lovely time. Plenty of things to do.

EROTICA   Mummy how do you spell "verging"?

AMMONIA   (*this gets her attention*) What? Virgin? What are you doing Erotica?

EROTICA   And "bonking" has two 'n's doesn't it?

AMMONIA   (*horrified*) Bonking???

EROTICA   I'm sending a message to a friend. I write it out and then a servant takes it to my friend who then chalks a reply back to me. It's all the rage. It's called "slating".

LUDICRUS   Proves my point completely. Even our own daughter has gone sex mad.

AMMONIA   (*grabs* EROTICA'S *slate*) Let me see that. (*She reads the message.*) "Hi, do you fancy meeting up later? I've a strong desire to do something verging on the ridiculous, you know how bonking mad I am." (*She hands back the slate to* EROTICA.) Harmless I suppose.

EROTICA   I didn't have enough room to write a longer message.

AMMONIA   (*helpfully*) Why don't you abbreviate the
            text? Then you could call it texting.

EROTICA   Oh mummy you are so funny! Whatever will
            you think of next? Texting?? (*She runs off
            giggling back into the house.*)

            (LURCIO *enters through the main door from
            the house. He is carrying two long poles,
            each with a pig's head stuck on it as well as
            a wicker basket containing fruit and wine.*)

LUDICRUS   Ah Lurcio, there you are. About time.

LURCIO   I know I'm a little late Master, it was the
            cook.

AMMONIA   Cook? What's wrong with her?

LURCIO   I had to bring her round.

LUDICRUS   Bring her round? What's the matter with
            her?

LURCIO   She's been mixing her drinks again. Her
            latest is the 'David and Goliath' special.
            One small shot and you're down and out!

LUDICRUS   (*despondently*) Staff problems are all I need.
            (*He exits into the house.*)

            (LURCIO *speaks to the audience.*)

LURCIO   Oh hello. I'm Lurcio, Head slave to my
            Master and Mistress here. Ludicrus Sextus
            and his wife Ammonia. The dynamic duo!

AMMONIA   What have you got there, Lurcio? (*She
            points at his pigs' heads.*)

LURCIO	These Mistress are my poles.
AMMONIA	(*investigating*) Yes but what are those hairy things?
LURCIO	The packed lunches. For your trip.
AMMONIA	I hope mine doesn't have mustard on it.
LURCIO	I thought you liked a bit of the hot stuff Mistress?
AMMONIA	(*tartly*) Not all the time Lurcio. (*She exits into the house.*)
LURCIO	Just between meals I suppose.
	(LURCIO *takes the food over to the stable. He accidentally drops a pig's head.* CORNEOUS *appears from the house carrying a bag.*)
LURCIO	Corneous, help me with this lot.
CORNEOUS	(*shaking his head*) Sorry, can't do that.
LURCIO	What do you mean? I'm not asking you to help me, I'm telling you. I'm head slave around here remember?
CORNEOUS	Union rules Lurcio.
LURCIO	What?
CORNEOUS	I'm a footman. Loading luggage, delivering messages, pulling carts – that's alright. Anything to do with feet is my job. But food (*Points at pigs' heads.*) is your job. Not my union you see. That's for a general household slave.

LURCIO	Don't be ridiculous.
CORNEOUS	Anything to do with feet, that's me.
LURCIO	Well try this for size. (*He kicks* CORNEOUS *up the backside.*)
CORNEOUS	Ow!!! (*He puts his bag on the cart.*)
	(AMMONIA *calls* CORNEOUS.)
AMMONIA	(*off*) Corneous? Come and carry my luggage.
CORNEOUS	Coming Mistress . . .
	(LURCIO *drops off the pigs' heads and basket into the stable.*)
LURCIO	Flaming cheek!! I'll give him feet. (*To audience.*) You just can't get the staff these days. Especially not with this lot. I was in a better cast when I broke my leg. Oh I need a bit of a sit down. All this running around . . . (*He sits down on his stone. We can see his underpants under his short toga. He desperately tries to hide this by pulling down the toga, crossing his legs, etc.*) Ooops! Sorry about that!

Now what was it I was going to tell you? I've got a shocking memory. Shocking! (*He suddenly remembers.*) Oh yes, let me put you in the picture. Let us familiarise ourselves. Here we all are in ancient Pompeii. (*He looks around him at the house.*) With the B&Q doors. You know where Pompeii is don't you? Italy, that's right. Imagine Italy looking like a long woman's leg with a high heel on the end. |

(*He demonstrates with his own leg.*) Well
Pompeii is about halfway up. Not quite high
enough to be interesting but quite racy all
the same.

Now as I said I am Lurcio, slave to Ludicrus
Sextus which as you may have guessed
stands for Ludicrus the sixth and not
Ludicrus Sexy!

I like to kick things off with the "Prologue".
Not only is it a quick way to get into the
fruity part of the plot but also it helps me to
fill you in with who is who, who does what
to who and to whom they does what to. And
in addition how. Which brings me back to
the fruity part. The "Prologue" today is all
about a handsome young slave who found
himself working alone in Pompeii . . . Now,
when he arrived the first thing he heard
was . . .

LUDICRUS   (*off*) I've tried everything with it but it's
gone all floppy!

LURCIO   Eh?

(LUDICRUS *comes out of the house. He is
fiddling about with his laurel crown.*)

LUDICRUS   Damned greenfly! (*He flicks a few insects
off and puts it on his head.*) Lurcio, Lurcio?
I need a quiet word.

LURCIO   (*stands up*) Here we go! (*To* LUDICRUS.) Of
course Master, fire away.

LUDICRUS   It's a rather delicate matter. (*He sits on the
stone.*)

LURCIO	Oh, one of them? I'm all ears. (*He sits on the stone beside him.*)
LUDICRUS	It concerns a subject close to my heart. One that I don't open up that often.
LURCIO	Oh yes? Your wallet?
LUDICRUS	(*making sure no one is listening*) I don't know which way to put it . . .
LURCIO	Oh dear. That old problem again. Well it's quite easy Master, first you . . .
LUDICRUS	Naturally I'm talking about certain ladies.
LURCIO	Naturally, but it's still the same . . .
LUDICRUS	Certain ladies that like to do things with us men. Are you with me Lurcio?
LURCIO	Certainly Master, if you're paying.
LUDICRUS	I am talking about . . .
LURCIO	I think we all know what you're talking about!
LUDICRUS	. . . a little bit of research for my Senate bill. (*He makes sure no one is within earshot.*) You see I have told my wife that I am off to Rome but I'm not really.
LURCIO	Oh yes? (*To the audience.*) The plot thickens . . .
LUDICRUS	I'm only telling you Lurcio because you are my servant and I trust you explicitly. You won't spill the beans will you?

LURCIO   Me? Spill the beans? Of course not. (*A beat.*) What beans Master?

LUDICRUS   Well I've taken a bit of a fancy to the woman who lives in that villa by the lake. The one with the high wall? Perhaps you've noticed her?

LURCIO   Suspenda? The well-known nymphomaniac and beauty? No, can't really say I've noticed her much . . .

LUDICRUS   Well, what I want you to do is send her this message from me asking her over for tea later today. (*He hands* LURCIO *a scroll.*)

LURCIO   For tea?

LUDICRUS   That's right and hopefully she'll stay for breakfast as well. (*He rubs his hands together at the excitement of his proposal.*)

LURCIO   I get the picture.

LUDICRUS   Of course it's all in the name of research.

LURCIO   Of course it is.

LUDICRUS   Now this is all very hush-hush, Lurcio.

LURCIO   Oh yes, hush-hush. (*To audience.*) Keep it to yourselves. Very hush-hush!

LUDICRUS   Ammonia and Erotica will be staying with my mother at Tedius in the countryside.

LURCIO   Mistress Botoxia? Right . . .

LUDICRUS   So it will be just between you and me and the beautiful Suspenda.

LURCIO	I see, just the three of us.
LUDICRUS	(*suddenly worried*) And there's my son Nausius of course.
LURCIO	Nausius? Well surely we don't want him in on it. He's so young and innocent.
LUDICRUS	Exactly. And that's the way I want him to stay. I don't want him knowing about Suspenda.
LURCIO	No, of course not.
LUDICRUS	I have recently noticed a change in my son, Lurcio. No longer does he care about his hobbies.
LURCIO	But his butterfly collection is legendary.
LUDICRUS	Indeed but he is no longer interested. Nowadays his attention is on bodies.
LURCIO	Bodies? Heavenly bodies?
LUDICRUS	No! Human bodies. Do you know what happened yesterday? I caught him in front of the mirror, stark naked, looking at himself. And what do you think he was doing?
LURCIO	I shudder to think Master.
LUDICRUS	He was reciting his love odes!
LURCIO	Well I never . . .
LUDICRUS	He is no longer a boy I fear. He is getting far too interested in the opposite sex. I want

you to keep an eye on him. Keep him away from certain women.

LURCIO   So I have to get you and this Mistress Suspenda together but at the same time keep your son away from women like her.

LUDICRUS   That's about the size of it Lurcio, yes.

LURCIO   Well, these things can cost you know . . .

LUDICRUS   (*hands* LURCIO *some coins*) Here's a little money for you to spend.

LURCIO   (*pockets the money*) I'm sure anything is possible. (*He holds out his hand for more.*)

LUDICRUS   (*gives him more coins*) Perhaps this will help.

LURCIO   (*pockets the money*) I'm sure I'll find something to distract your son, Master.

LUDICRUS   As long as it's not women Lurcio!

LURCIO   No, I'll leave that to you.

LUDICRUS   As long as you understand your responsibilities or else it's the . . . lions!

LURCIO   (*nervously*) The lions . . . oh yes . . . oh dear!

LUDICRUS   Now I shall just go and collect my personal belongings and then I must be off. (*Taps his nose.*) Remember, mum's the word.

LURCIO   (*taps his nose*) Oh yes.

(LUDICRUS *exits into the house passing*
CORNEOUS *coming out of the house. He
carries a large wicker basket that looks as if
it has come from the kitchen.* LURCIO *seizes
on this oversight.*)

LURCIO   Oh yes. I see you carry stuff from the
              kitchen when the Mistress asks you to.

CORNEOUS   Certainly not. I'm a footman, as I told you
              before.

LURCIO   Then what have you got in here? (*He opens
              the basket lid with such force that it hits*
              CORNEOUS *on the nose.*)

CORNEOUS   Ow!!

              (LURCIO *pulls out various ladies shoes out of
              the basket. He reacts.*)

CORNEOUS   Anything to do with feet you see.

LURCIO   Cobblers!! (*Slams lid of basket shut.*)

              (CORNEOUS *puts the basket into the cart and
              then exits into the house passing* AMMONIA.
              She walks over to LURCIO.)

AMMONIA   Lurcio! I would like a word.

LURCIO   (*to audience*) Oh I am popular today. (*To*
              AMMONIA.) Yes, Mistress.

              (AMMONIA *sits on the stone facing audience.*
              LURCIO *joins her.*)

AMMONIA   I'm not happy with the way things have
              been going lately.

LURCIO	It's Cook isn't it? She drinks everything in sight. She'll have to go.
AMMONIA	I'm talking about the general running of the household.
LURCIO	Oh?
AMMONIA	A certain lazy streak has been creeping in.
LURCIO	What?? Well just point him out Mistress and I'll show him the door. We don't want that type around here.
AMMONIA	I'm talking about you Lurcio.
LURCIO	Me?
AMMONIA	Yes you. Last week you were bathing in my bath.
LURCIO	But we're allowed to Mistress. Once a month. Servants' concession.
AMMONIA	Yes but not at the same time that I'm in it!
LURCIO	That was a misunderstanding Mistress. I could have sworn you said "Lurcio, come and try me".
AMMONIA	Dry me is what I said Lurcio.
LURCIO	Yes Mistress. Silly me.
AMMONIA	Things have been getting very shoddy around here and I hold you responsible. You are the head slave of my household. Just.
LURCIO	What do you mean? Just?

AMMONIA   There are other slaves waiting to take your
               job.

LURCIO   (*stands up*) Other slaves? Who'd want my
               job?

AMMONIA   Corneous for one.

LURCIO   Corneous? That little toad? I knew it, I
               could see it in his eyes.

AMMONIA   See what?

LURCIO   Power, Mistress. He won't be happy at just
               being head slave. Oh no, he's got aims for
               higher things.

AMMONIA   To be one of my eunuchs?

LURCIO   No, no I don't think he's cut out for that.

AMMONIA   Well at least he's efficient, which is a lot
               more than I can say for you. I have decided
               to give you one final chance Lurcio.

LURCIO   Thank you Mistress.

AMMONIA   You must pull your sandal-straps up.

LURCIO   Consider them up Mistress.

AMMONIA   Or else I shall have no alternative but to
               have you thrown to the . . . lions! (*She exits
               into the house.*)

LURCIO   (*nervously*) Those lions again. Oh dear. (*To
               audience.*) But what about my pride? Come
               on, come on. Lions? Pride? Oh forget it!
               Please yourselves! I told the director that

was a lame gag but would he listen? Too
busy knocking back his gin and tonics!

(CORNEOUS *brings out another basket.*
LURCIO *investigates.*)

LURCIO   And what do we have here this time?

CORNEOUS   These are the Mistress's wigs. (*He opens the
              basket and holds up a long-haired wig.*)

LURCIO   I see and the connection with feet is?

              (CORNEOUS *looks stumped for a moment.*)

CORNEOUS   (*inspired*) Each hair is a foot long!

LURCIO   Pathetic! Anyway, hair today, gone
              tomorrow.

CORNEOUS   Not me mate. I'm going to the top. (*He exits
              into the stable with the basket.*)

              (LUDICRUS, AMMONIA *and* EROTICA *enter
              from the house.* EROTICA *is still composing
              messages on her slate.*)

LUDICRUS   (*to* AMMONIA) Right, are you ready my dear?

AMMONIA   As I'll ever be. I still can't see why I can't
              come with you to Rome.

LUDICRUS   As I've already explained, you'll be far
              happier with my mother.

AMMONIA   But what shall I do? I hate the countryside.

LUDICRUS   Go down to the stable, select a strong
              animal . . .

LURCIO   (*sotto*) Get something between your legs and
              enjoy yourself.

AMMONIA   I hate that kind of thing. I'm a hopeless
              rider. I can never get up into the saddle.

LURCIO   Perhaps the stable lads could gather around
              and make a few suggestions, Mistress?

LUDICRUS   Lurcio's quite right my dear. I'm sure
              there'll be plenty of offers to get you
              mounted.

              (CORNEOUS *enters from the stable.*)

AMMONIA   I suppose I could give it a go. (*To* LURCIO.)
              And when I return I shall expect things to be
              in order.

LURCIO   I shall do my best Mistress.

              (CORNEOUS *pushes in front of* LURCIO *and
              speaks to* AMMONIA.)

CORNEOUS   (*obsequiously*) You can rely on me,
              Mistress.

LURCIO   (*to* CORNEOUS) Watch it mate! I'm head slave
              and don't forget it.

CORNEOUS   Not for long.

              (EROTICA *gives her slate to* CORNEOUS.)

EROTICA   While I'm away Corneous, can you make
              sure you deliver this?

CORNEOUS   You can rely on me, young Mistress.

EROTICA   Thank you so much. Make sure my friend
           gets the message. (*She gives* CORNEOUS *a big
           wink unseen by the others.* LURCIO *does see
           it however and is curious.*)

CORNEOUS   Yes Mistress. (*He winks back.*)

LUDICRUS   Now, let us go down to the terminus.
           Corneous, you know what to do.

CORNEOUS   Straight away Master. (*He goes into the
           stable.*)

LURCIO   (*mimicking* CORNEOUS) Straight away
           Master. (*To audience.*) Little upstart. I'll
           have to watch him. Make sure he doesn't get
           his foot on the ladder. Get it? Foot on the
           ladder? Oh never mind . . .

           (CORNEOUS *comes out of the stable pushing
           the cart now loaded with the family's
           baskets and bags.*)

LUDICRUS   Right, off we go.

           (*They are about to exit when there is a
           distant roar and shake of a volcano. They
           all react by wobbling and shaking and
           holding onto anything they can.*)

AMMONIA   I'm sure that volcano is going to erupt one
           day.

EROTICA   Mummy I'm frightened.

           (*Another roar, but much more distant and
           quieter than before. They all look at each
           other in desperation.* LURCIO *decides to sort
           it out.*)

LURCIO   Oh dear! It's pathetic. (*Into the wings.*)
                Can't you make it a bit louder? It's meant to
                be Vesuvius mush! Not a fart in a bath. (*To
                audience.*) Honestly these stagehands, half-
                asleep most of the time. I don't know why
                we bother.

                (*There is now a much louder and violent
                roar of a volcano.*)

LURCIO   That's better. Now let's get on with it . . .

AMMONIA   (*picking up her cue*) I'm sure that volcano is
                going to erupt one day.

EROTICA   Mummy I'm frightened.

AMMONIA   Don't worry Erotica. It's the big ones you
                have to watch.

LURCIO   (*to the audience*) She'd know.

LUDICRUS   The Gods will protect us. Nothing to get
                excited about. Vesuvius only sends out the
                odd tremor.

AMMONIA   (*sotto*) A bit like you.

LUDICRUS   Now we must get on our way.

                (AMMONIA *sits on the cart and* CORNEOUS
                *strains at the heavy load he has to push and
                hits the wall. They all exit through the iron
                gate.*)

LURCIO   Off you go. Have a good time. Byeeee . . .
                (*To audience.*) Now where was I? (*He sits
                down on the stone.*) Oh yes, the "Prologue".
                Now there was this handsome young slave
                who came to Pompeii . . .

(SENNA *the old hag Soothsayer rushes on through the iron gate, wailing.*)

SENNA   Nigh, nigh and thrice nigh!

LURCIO   Oh dear, it's Senna the Soothsayer. A little of her goes a long way. (*To* SENNA.) How are you dear?

SENNA   (*tugs at his sleeve*) I must warn you of strange happenings.

LURCIO   Oh yes?

SENNA   I had one in my bed last night.

LURCIO   What? A strange happening?

SENNA   A visitation.

LURCIO   That would be strange for you.

SENNA   It warned me of evil things that are going to happen to you.

LURCIO   That's right, give me the good news why don't you?

SENNA   It is meant as a warning of things to come.

LURCIO   Here we go . . .

SENNA   Let me look in my crystal ball.

LURCIO   Where have you hidden it?

SENNA   It's in here somewhere. (*She delves into the top of her dress and starts searching.*)

LURCIO   Careful, careful. Make sure you get the right
              one.

SENNA   (*producing a glass ball*) Here we are. (*Looks
              into it.*) Oh woe, woe and thrice woe!

LURCIO   What is it? What is it?

SENNA   There's going to be a severe snowstorm in
              Rome. A big freeze. Death to many. Icicles
              everywhere. The gladiators will wish that
              their armour was not so fashionably short at
              the thigh.

LURCIO   Why?

SENNA   Because it's going to freeze their bollo . . .

LURCIO   (*snatching the ball*) That's the wrong
              ball you twit!! It's the cheap snow globe
              souvenir the Master gave you last year.
              Have another dig dear.

SENNA   (*produces another ball from her dress*)
              Maybe this time I won't see any snow.

LURCIO   Never mind the weather forecast. What's
              happening to me in the future? Do I ever get
              freed?

SENNA   (*gazes into ball*) Oh nigh, nigh and thrice
              nigh . . .

LURCIO   What does it say?

SENNA   (*concentrating on the crystal ball*) Speak to
              me oh ball! Speak to me oh ball!

LURCIO   Well I've heard of talking balls but can we
              get to the prophecy please?

SENNA	You are going to receive a visitation.
LURCIO	As long as it's not the same one who calls on you.
SENNA	A beautiful blonde nubile girl.
LURCIO	Oh? Now you're talking . . .
SENNA	She's going to do anything you desire.
LURCIO	Sounds like my kind of girl.
SENNA	(*looks deeper into ball*) But beware!
LURCIO	I knew there had to be a catch.
SENNA	She comes with treacherous, dangerous, villainous . . .
LURCIO	She can bring the whole family for all I care.
SENNA	. . . men chasing her. You must be careful.
LURCIO	Don't worry, I like a little competition. As long as I win.
SENNA	Also I see treachery afoot.
LURCIO	That'll be Corneous. He's got a thing about feet.
SENNA	I see death for him. His fate is indescribable, it is so ghastly.
LURCIO	A sort of feet beyond death? (*To audience.*) . . . Feet beyond death? Come on, come on keep up! Don't doze off at the back. Oh I don't know why I bother . . .

SENNA   I must go. Oh woe, woe and thrice woe.
             (*She exits through the iron gate.*)

LURCIO   There's no business like woe business!
             Silly old bag. (*To audience.*) She always
             gets her predictions wrong. The only people
             who benefit are bookies. No, don't laugh.
             It's very sad. She has a lonely life. Always
             knowing in advance that she's going to
             be wrong. But she can't help it poor soul.
             She's repressed you see. You know what I
             mean, don't you? Ever since she was a girl
             she's had this thing against men. But they
             kept pushing it away. No, don't laugh. It's
             wicked to mock the afflicted.

             Well, anyway what a day! Fancy my Master
             wanting to meet this Suspenda woman?
             Oh don't get me wrong, she's a looker all
             right. Gorgeous! Every time I go down to
             the market I see her sunbathing naked in her
             garden. That's as long as I've remembered
             to bring the apple crate to stand on. High
             wall, you see.

             Anyway, I can see why he's interested in
             her. There's a rumour going round that she's
             pretty easy to get romantically involved
             with, if you take my meaning. Around here
             she's known as Madeira, because she's a
             piece of cake.

             Let's have a look at this letter. (*He takes out
             the scroll and unrolls it.*) See what the silly
             old fool has said. (*Reads from scroll.*) "Dear
             Suspenda", I suppose that's the best way to
             start it. You can hardly say Dear "Gagging-
             for-it" can you? "Dear Suspenda, You don't
             know me but I know you. I was wondering
             whether you were doing anything this
             weekend? If not, could you come over to

my place and squeeze my . . ." (*Looks out at audience and reacts.*) Hold it! Hold it! We'll have none of that thank you very much. (*Back to scroll.*) "If not, could you come over to my place and squeeze my presence into your busy schedule? I would be very grateful. Yours in anticipation, Ludicrus Sextus. PS: Bring an overnight bag." (*He rolls the scroll up.*)

Do you think that's a bit too strong? From what I've heard she doesn't need encouragement anyway. You know the sort. A couple of drinks and she's anybody's, a few more and she's everybody's. She's the original good time had by all!

(CORNEOUS *returns through the iron gate pulling the empty cart. He wheels it back into the stable.*)

LURCIO
You're back then?

CORNEOUS
The terminus is as far as I go. If the Master had wanted me to go to Rome, there would have been expenses to consider.

LURCIO
Always on the make. Anyway, there's something I want you to do.

CORNEOUS
It'll have to wait. It's time for my break. (*He accidentally points to where his wristwatch would be.* LURCIO *picks up on this.*)

LURCIO
They hadn't been invented back then!

CORNEOUS
(*trying not to laugh*) Oh right, yes anyway . . . My break . . .

LURCIO   You can have that later. I want you to
            deliver this letter.

CORNEOUS   I'm not delivering anything for you.

LURCIO   Don't be cheeky! You will deliver this letter
            and like it.

CORNEOUS   Shan't!

LURCIO   Shall!

CORNEOUS   Shan't! And whilst we're about it Lurcio,
            I think you should know that the Mistress
            isn't too pleased with the way things have
            been going lately.

LURCIO   Yes and I wonder who's been telling her?

CORNEOUS   I intend to be head slave around here pretty
            soon.

LURCIO   Over my dead body.

CORNEOUS   If necessary, yes.

LURCIO   You don't frighten me mate. I know your
            sort only too well. I eat people like you for
            breakfast.

CORNEOUS   Roman berries? Strong and potent?

LURCIO   No, prunes. You're nothing but a load of hot
            air!

CORNEOUS   I shall ignore your remarks and take my
            break. (*He looks at where his wristwatch
            would be again and then realises his
            mistake.*) For which I am already late.
            (*Starts to exit into the house.*)

LURCIO	In that case I shall deliver the Master's letter to the beautiful Suspenda myself.
CORNEOUS	(*this stops him*) Suspenda? The well-known nymphomaniac and beauty?
LURCIO	The very same.
CORNEOUS	You didn't say the letter was for her.
LURCIO	What difference does it make? You don't want to deliver it.
CORNEOUS	Perhaps I was a little hasty before.
LURCIO	Oh yes? Changed your mind, have you?
CORNEOUS	But why would the Master be writing to Suspenda, the well-known nymphomaniac and beauty?
LURCIO	None of your business. Now, are you going to deliver this letter or not?
CORNEOUS	(*snatches the scroll*) Yes.
LURCIO	You must promise to go straight there. (*Snatches the scroll back.*)
CORNEOUS	Nothing will stop me. (*Snatches the scroll back.*)
LURCIO	And you must not read the letter on the way. (*Snatches the scroll back.*)
CORNEOUS	My eyes are sealed. (*Snatches the scroll and closes his eyes.*)
LURCIO	And you must not tell anyone about this. (*Snatches the scroll back.*)

CORNEOUS	My mouth is sealed. (*Snatches the scroll back.*)
LURCIO	That'll make a change. Off you go then.
	(CORNEOUS *turns to leave and walks straight into the well with a loud thud.*)
CORNEOUS	Ow!!!
LURCIO	You can open your eyes now you idiot!
	(CORNEOUS *moves to the iron gate.* LURCIO *pops into the cupboard under the stairs.*)
LURCIO	Hang on. (*He brings out a small wooden box.*) You'll probably need this. Grab yourself an eyeful on the way in.
CORNEOUS	(*takes box*) Right. (*He exits through the iron gate.*)
LURCIO	(*to audience*) Well you've got to make the trip worthwhile for these footmen haven't you? Now where was I . . .
	(VOLUPTUA, *a pretty, shapely slave girl rushes in through the iron gate. She is out of breath and frightened.*)
LURCIO	Hello, hello and what have we here? An Amazonian delivery?
VOLUPTUA	Please, you must help me! I need assistance.
LURCIO	Don't scream too loud girl. We don't want everybody in the street coming to your aid. I'm here. Now what's your problem?
VOLUPTUA	I am a slave on the run.

LURCIO   Oh, liberated eh?

VOLUPTUA   I have escaped from the slave galley in the
              docks.

LURCIO   The 'Long Oar'?

VOLUPTUA   Yes but they are after me. You must help.

LURCIO   Hang on, hang on. Who are after you?

VOLUPTUA   The evil Captain Treacherus and his men.

              (LURCIO *is terrified at the very mention of
              this man's name.*)

LURCIO   (*nervously*) The evil Captain Treacherus
              . . . listen dear, you've come to the wrong
              place. We don't want any escaped slaves
              here. We're all trying to get out ourselves.
              You should see our escape committee, you
              have to book well ahead. I've got an attempt
              coming up two years on Friday.

VOLUPTUA   You won't help me?

LURCIO   You're better off on the run. You've already
              escaped. You've done the hard part now just
              keep going.

              (CAPTAIN TREACHERUS *can be heard shouting
              orders in the distance.*)

TREACHERUS   (*off*) You men, search that house. Move!
              Move!

              (*The sound of marching men is heard.*)

VOLUPTUA   Help me escape and I will do anything you
              desire.

LURCIO	It's very tempting but I don't feel . . .
VOLUPTUA	Think of all the fun we could have together. (*She runs her hand down his thigh.*)
LURCIO	Yes but . . .
VOLUPTUA	Just you and little me. (*She pouts her lips.*)
LURCIO	No, you must leave . . .
	(CAPTAIN TREACHERUS *is heard getting nearer.*)
TREACHERUS	(*off*) You, Kretinus. Come with me. We'll search this house first. Move!
	(*More sound of marching men.*)
VOLUPTUA	I would do anything for you.
LURCIO	Anything?
VOLUPTUA	As long as it gives you pleasure.
LURCIO	Quick! Get into this sack. (*He picks up a hessian rubbish sack.*)
VOLUPTUA	Kinky, eh? (*She starts to climb into the sack.*)
LURCIO	(*pushing her in*) Get in! Get in!
VOLUPTUA	I can't! It stinks! (*She tries to get out.*)
LURCIO	(*pushing her back in*) What do you expect? It's a rubbish sack.
VOLUPTUA	(*as she disappears*) Urgh!! It's revolting!

(CAPTAIN TREACHERUS *and his thug sidekick*
KRETINUS *enter through the iron gate.*
TREACHERUS *is a ruthless slave trader,*
KRETINUS *is an idiot. They are both wearing*
uniforms. TREACHERUS *carries a sword.*)

TREACHERUS   Let's see what we have here Kretinus. (*He*
points his sword at LURCIO.)

KRETINUS   Your sword Captain?

TREACHERUS   (*waves his sword*) Not this you fool. (*Points*
at LURCIO.) Him!

LURCIO   (*with as much cool as he can muster*) Good
morning gentlemen. Can I help you?

TREACHERUS   We're looking for an escaped slave.

KRETINUS   (*standing behind* LURCIO *and lifting up his*
toga) I don't think this is her, Captain.

TREACHERUS   Of course it's not you idiot!

LURCIO   An escaped slave you say?

TREACHERUS   That's right. Have you seen anyone
suspicious around here?

LURCIO   It would be quicker for me to give you a
list of those who aren't suspicious. They're
a funny lot here you know. You should see
Cook.

TREACHERUS   Interesting but quite irrelevant. I am Captain
Treacherus the infamous slave trader.

(VOLUPTUA *in the sack shakes a little. No*
one notices except for LURCIO *who stops her*
with his foot.)

TREACHERUS   Perhaps you've heard of me?

LURCIO   Something or other, yes.

TREACHERUS   Everyone's heard of Captain Treacherus,
                haven't they Kretinus? (*He gives an evil
                chuckle.*)

KRETINUS   Oh yes. (*Joins in the laughter.*) Absolutely.
                (*Looks totally blank.*) Who?

TREACHERUS   (*jabs him with tip of sword*) Me you
                buffoon!

KRETINUS   Oh yes.

TREACHERUS   (*to* LURCIO) I am known throughout the
                Roman Empire as ruthless and evil but
                underneath it all I am . . .

LURCIO   A great big pussycat?

TREACHERUS   . . . far worse than my reputation suggests.
                You see, there's only one thing in the world
                that I can't abide.

LURCIO   Oh really? Do tell.

TREACHERUS   Slaves. I utterly detest them.

LURCIO   Aren't you in the wrong business then?

TREACHERUS   Unless they're working on my galleys. (*He
                circles* LURCIO.) Tell me, are you a slave?

LURCIO   Yes but I'm accredited you know.

TREACHERUS   I see. Well you may have protection here but
                if I ever find you hanging around the docks

I'll book you in for a Mediterranean cruise with no sun.

LURCIO   Oh dear . . .

TREACHERUS   Just loads of oars going in and out, up and down, in and out . . .

LURCIO   (*brightening up*) That doesn't sound too bad.

TREACHERUS   I said "oars"!

LURCIO   Oh, oars. Right . . .

TREACHERUS   Tell me then, who is your Master?

LURCIO   I am head slave to Ludicrus Sextus.

TREACHERUS   Ludicrus Sextus? Now where have I heard that name before?

KRETINUS   This bloke just told you, Captain.

TREACHERUS   (*to* KRETINUS) Halfwit! (*To* LURCIO.) Isn't Ludicrus Sextus a Senator?

LURCIO   Well, yes he is since you mention it. A very powerful Senator. And I think he'll object to your intrusion on his property.

TREACHERUS   Will he indeed? Well he doesn't worry me because he is the same Senator who is trying to clamp down on sex in our society, isn't he?

LURCIO   I wouldn't say that he was trying to clamp it exactly. Just stop the flow a little.

TREACHERUS   If his new bill goes through, a great many of
              us will find our fun has stopped.

LURCIO   I'm sure he could make one or two
              exceptions in your case.

TREACHERUS   They're all hypocrites these politicians.
              He would be just the sort to hide a slave.
              Especially if she's a young pretty girl. (*He
              puts his sword to* LURCIO's *throat.*) So where
              is she?

LURCIO   I don't know.

TREACHERUS   You're lying.

LURCIO   I am not!

TREACHERUS   She is somewhere in this house. I will count
              to three and if you don't tell me I shall cut
              your throat from ear to ear.

LURCIO   'ere 'ere . . .

TREACHERUS   One!

LURCIO   Now let's not be hasty.

TREACHERUS   Two!

LURCIO   I know nothing.

KRETINUS   That's what he keeps saying about me.

TREACHERUS   Shut up Kretinus!

LURCIO   Yes, shut up Kretinus.

TREACHERUS   Three!

(LURCIO *drops to his knees.*)

LURCIO   (*petrified*) Please don't hurt me. I beg you! I
            plead for my life. I plead for mercy.

TREACHERUS You miserable specimen!

LURCIO   Yes I'm a miserable pleader!

TREACHERUS You have not given me the information that
            I asked for. I shall cut your throat you scum!

LURCIO   Oh dear. It's scum to this! (*To audience.*)
            Come on, come on. I'm working my
            backside off here. Give me a bit of
            encouragement. What did you expect?
            Culture? (*To* TREACHERUS.) Look, can't we
            discuss this? (*He gets up off his knees.*)

TREACHERUS No we can't! (VOLUPTUA, *inside the sack,
            moves.*) Wait a minute, that sack. I'm sure it
            moved. (*He goes to investigate.*)

LURCIO   Surely you're mistaken?

TREACHERUS Is the slave girl in there?

LURCIO   In there? Good gracious no. All you'll find
            in there is last month's rubbish.

TREACHERUS Last month's rubbish? (*Turns his head away
            from the smell.*)

LURCIO   The bin men are on strike.

TREACHERUS (*starts to open sack*) I saw something move.

LURCIO   That would be the rats.

TREACHERUS Rats!! (*He drops the sack and steps back.*)

KRETINUS   (*alarmed*) Oooh rats!! Where? Where?

LURCIO   Oh yes, there's a lot of rats around here.
                (*Sotto.*) Present company included.

TREACHERUS   I detest rats almost as much as slaves.

LURCIO   I dare say you've got plenty of both on your
                galleys.

TREACHERUS   I suggest you spend more time cleaning
                up your own backyard, slave, than you
                do trying to make clever remarks. Just
                remember you may be safe here but if I ever
                catch you down at the docks . . .

LURCIO   You'll send me on a Mediterranean cruise
                with no sun?

TREACHERUS   You've got it. Come along Kretinus, we
                shall find no slave girl here.

KRETINUS   (*helpfully*) Perhaps she's hiding back on the
                slave ship, Captain?

TREACHERUS   Fully chained up I suppose? You moron!
                Move!

                (TREACHERUS *and* KRETINUS *exit through the
                iron gate.*)

LURCIO   Phew! That was close.

VOLUPTUA   (*from inside sack*) Can I come out now?

LURCIO   Yes, the coast's clear. Old hatchet features
                has left.

(Lurcio helps Voluptua climb out of the sack. At one stage his face is on the same level as her chest.)

LURCIO   Nice to see you three again.

(Voluptua climbs out of the sack.)

VOLUPTUA   You were very brave.

LURCIO   Think nothing of it.

VOLUPTUA   You saved my life.

LURCIO   Just one of those things.

VOLUPTUA   In return I shall do anything for you.

LURCIO   Well I suppose I was pretty heroic wasn't I?

(Voluptua rushes up to Lurcio and smothers him with passionate kisses. He indulges but then resists her.)

LURCIO   No! No, get off! Get away!

VOLUPTUA   You do not like me?

LURCIO   No, no . . . well . . .

(He pulls her back towards him for more kisses but again ends up rejecting her.)

VOLUPTUA   What is wrong?

LURCIO   It's the smell of all that rotting rubbish. You must go to the bathroom and bathe. *(He points up the steps to the bathroom door.)*

VOLUPTUA   And you will join me?

LURCIO	Try and stop me. By the way, what is your name? Mine is Lurcio.
VOLUPTUA	They call me Voluptua.
LURCIO	(*admiring her*) I bet they do.
VOLUPTUA	(*moves up steps*) Please don't be long Lurcio . . .
LURCIO	Oh, call me Lurky.
VOLUPTUA	Alright . . . Lurky. I so want to express my gratitude. (*She gives him a smouldering look.*)
LURCIO	Just go and tickle your fancy on a geyser or two.
VOLUPTUA	There's only one geezer for me. (*She blows* LURCIO *a kiss and then exits into the bathroom giggling.*)
LURCIO	(*to audience*) Well I never. This is a turn-up for the books and make no mistake. What shall I do? I can't let the poor girl down. She is full of gratitude and wants me to feel it and, let's not quibble about this, I want to feel it.
	(*He starts walking up the steps towards the bathroom.*)
	I'll see you lot later on then. Talk amongst yourselves. Pass around the mints, read your programmes . . .
	(LURCIO *is about to enter the bathroom when* NAUSIUS, *his Master's innocent son, enters*

through the iron gate. He is in a distraught state. He spots LURCIO.)

NAUSIUS   Oh Lurcio! Thank goodness you're here.

LURCIO   Nausius! What a surprise. (*To audience.*)
               Nausius, Ludicrus's offspring and right now
               I wish that he'd do just that and spring off
               somewhere else. (*To* NAUSIUS.) How are you
               young Master?

               (LURCIO *comes back down the steps.*)

NAUSIUS   Most unhappy, Lurcio. That is why I just
               had to find you.

LURCIO   Oh yes . . .

NAUSIUS   I have been down at the docks . . .

LURCIO   (*concerned*) The docks?

NAUSIUS   And as I walked along the quayside I saw
               this beautiful girl.

LURCIO   There's a lot of them down there young
               Master. You must be careful. Your father
               wouldn't like it. I suppose she asked you for
               money?

NAUSIUS   She did not ask me for money Lurcio but
               even if she had I would have gladly paid it.
               Just to gaze into her eyes.

LURCIO   Listen if you're going to pay at least get
               value for money. If all you want is to gaze
               into somebody's eyes, gaze into Cook's.
               That's if you can prise them open.

NAUSIUS   I would gladly have gazed at all her body but her eyes were all I could see through the gap. She was a slave on a galley. (*Dreamily.*) I fell in love with her there and then.

LURCIO   Taking a bit of a chance weren't you? If all you could see were these eyes? The rest of her body might have been a man's.

NAUSIUS   She whispered to me "Help me escape and I will do anything you desire."

LURCIO   Really? Fancy that? (*With one eye on the bathroom door.*) She certainly knows how to use her feminine charm, does that one.

NAUSIUS   I was putty in her hands Lurcio. She was so beautiful. I just had to save her.

LURCIO   So what did you do?

NAUSIUS   I jumped aboard the ship and before the guards could stop me I climbed up the rigging to the top of the mast. (*A beat.*) You get a lovely view from up there you know.

LURCIO   I bet everyone got a pretty good view from below too!

NAUSIUS   Anyway my diversion worked. This beautiful slave took advantage of the guards chasing after me and leapt off the galley and into freedom.

LURCIO   And what happened to you?

NAUSIUS   I climbed down the rigging and displayed my credentials . . .

LURCIO   I bet you did.

NAUSIUS   . . . and they let me go. But I cannot find the
               beautiful slave girl anywhere. You haven't
               seen her have you Lurcio?

LURCIO   Me? Good heavens no. (*With one eye on the
               bathroom door.*) Why would a girl like that
               come here?

NAUSIUS   (*sits down on step*) I must find her Lurcio,
               she is the light of my life. I have already
               written a love ode about her. Perhaps you
               would care to read it?

LURCIO   Maybe another time young Master . . .

NAUSIUS   I thought you would. (*Unrolls a scroll of
               paper and hands it to* LURCIO *who sits down
               beside him and reads it out.*)

LURCIO   "She's warm and she is gorgeous, and
               keeps me on my wits . . ." (*He looks out at
               the audience with a knowing look before
               continuing.*) "I long to hold her in my arms
               and squeeze her lovely . . . toes?"

NAUSIUS   I couldn't think of a suitable rhyme there.

LURCIO   You must be the only one who can't! Look,
               can't you take an interest in the simpler
               things of life. Take your mind off girls. Start
               collecting butterflies again?

NAUSIUS   I am not in the slightest bit interested in
               butterflies Lurcio. I want to know about the
               fairer sex. You must tell me all you know.

LURCIO   I don't think that is a very good idea young
               Master.

NAUSIUS   Why not? I have a couple of minutes spare.

               (LURCIO *reacts*.)

LURCIO   Yes, yes I'll do the jokes if you don't mind!
               (*To audience*.) Honestly these young actors!
               Always trying to steal the scene. Never
               heard of feedlines, always punchline mad.
               (*To* NAUSIUS.) Look, this is not the time. You
               will discover these pleasures in due course.
               Why rush these things? Especially this
               weekend?

NAUSIUS   I'll do anything for you Lurcio, if only
               you'll tell me a few facts.

LURCIO   No, young Master. It is not my place. Your
               father would not like it.

NAUSIUS   I would even ask my parents to free you.
               I'm sure they wouldn't mind you going.

LURCIO   (*tempted*) Well . . .

NAUSIUS   Your freedom for my initiation.

LURCIO   Well perhaps . . . No, no, no. It's the lions
               you see.

NAUSIUS   The lions?

LURCIO   They're a hungry lot this time of year and I
               don't fancy being their dinner.

NAUSIUS   But Lurcio . . .

LURCIO   (*stands up*) No I'm sorry young Master, my
               mind is made up. Absolutely no way. You'll
               just have to wait until your wedding night.

NAUSIUS   My wedding night?

LURCIO   Yes that's when these things have a habit of
             coming together.

NAUSIUS   But when will my wedding night be Lurcio?

LURCIO   Who cares? As long as it's not tonight. (*With
             an eye on the bathroom door.*) A thought has
             just occurred young Master.

NAUSIUS   Yes?

LURCIO   When your beautiful slave girl escaped, did
             anyone go after her?

NAUSIUS   (*thinks hard*) Yes, I did.

LURCIO   I know that but did any of the guards chase
             her?

NAUSIUS   Yes, the Captain himself and some of his
             men.

LURCIO   Then has it not occurred to you that your
             beloved has been recaptured and is once
             more a prisoner on the galley?

NAUSIUS   (*alarmed*) Good gracious! Of course! I must
             get back there Lurcio and rescue her again.
             (*He stands up and runs to the iron gate.*)

LURCIO   And be sure to have clean underwear on.

NAUSIUS   Why?

LURCIO   When you go frigging up the rigging!

             (NAUSIUS *exits.*)

LURCIO   (*to audience*) That'll get him out the way.
                  Well he's young isn't he? He'll learn but
                  I'm not going to be the one to teach him.
                  Not with those lions about.

                  Now where was I? Oh yes . . . The
                  "Prologue". (*Considers this.*) Oh sod the
                  "Prologue". Voluptua!! (*Moves to bottom of
                  stairs and stops.*) I've just had a thought.
                  Why don't I put on my best togs? I have just
                  the toga to wear. (*He exits into the house.*)

                  (VOLUPTUA, *now wearing only a towel,
                  comes out of the bathroom and stands at the
                  top of the steps.*)

VOLUPTUA   Lurky? Oh Lurky?

LURCIO   (*off*) Er . . . yes.

VOLUPTUA   Where are you?

LURCIO   (*off*) I'm just changing into something more
                  comfortable.

VOLUPTUA   Are you coming up to keep me company in
                  this great big bath?

LURCIO   (*off*) Of course. I'll be up there in a minute.
                  Go and boil some more water.

VOLUPTUA   Wait till I get you to the boil! Don't be long
                  now. (*She exits into the bathroom.*)

                  (LURCIO *enters from inside the house. He's
                  struggling to put on his new toga.*)

LURCIO   (*to audience*) Honestly!! You'd think they'd
                  give her a few more lines so I'd have time to

change! Trouble with this lot, they all want
to get down the pub . . .

(*He pulls his new toga down and makes
himself presentable. It's longer than the
old one and has a bright sash on it that
will periodically cause him problems as he
wraps it around his arms, etc, during any
physical activity.*)

Anyway, what do you think? (*He gives a
twirl.*) Does it suit me? What do you mean I
haven't got the figure? I work out you know.
My legs are notorious down at the gym.
When I do the splits, they call it "Lurcio's
legendary leg-openers!"

(*He starts for the steps when* Suspenda,
arrives at the iron gate. She is ravishing and
Lurcio *is stunned.*)

LURCIO   (*to audience*) Oh my goodness!! It's her!
She's come. Suspenda, the well-known
nymphomaniac and beauty. I can't believe
it. This sort of thing only happens in
scrolls. (*To* Suspenda.) Hello there Mistress
Suspenda. Please do come in.

(*She walks towards* Lurcio.)

SUSPENDA   You recognise me?

LURCIO   Of course. I knew it was you as soon as I
saw your arse . . . ass. (*He looks off stage
into the street.*)

SUSPENDA   Would you please inform your Master,
Ludicrus Sextus, that I have arrived.

LURCIO He has been detained Mistress but has given me instructions to look after you.

SUSPENDA I see.

LURCIO I take it you received his note?

SUSPENDA Indeed. I read it once and came over as soon as I could.

LURCIO (*to audience*) See what I mean? Keen! (*To* SUSPENDA.) I trust our junior footman Corneous was courteous.

SUSPENDA Hmm . . . slightly over familiar perhaps.

LURCIO Where is he now?

SUSPENDA Still at my house.

LURCIO But why has he not returned with you, Mistress? (*Pointedly.*) You haven't given him a job I hope.

SUSPENDA He's fixing my garden wall. For some reason he was on it when it collapsed. Can't think why.

LURCIO (*to audience*) I can. Trying to get a better foothold. Get it? Foothold? Oh never mind.

SUSPENDA Your Master's letter was most interesting. Most forward. I like a man to be forward. (*Lustily.*) If you've got it, get it out is what I say. (*She lets out a cackling laugh.*)

LURCIO Indeed. (*To audience.*) Goodness, no wonder they call her Madeira. Piece of cake? This is more like a ten course feast! (*To* SUSPENDA.)

I thought perhaps something to eat first? My Master keeps an excellent meat table.

SUSPENDA   Not for me thank you, my appetite is for something more carnal than carvery. (*She lets out another cackling laugh.*)

LURCIO   (*reacts*) We could do with her in the audience! (*To* SUSPENDA.) Yes, well one can eat any old time.

SUSPENDA   I like to eat after . . .

LURCIO   Oh I agree. Much more civilised.

SUSPENDA   . . . the first three or four love sessions. I find it so revitalising.

LURCIO   (*to audience*) You'd need a bit of revitalising after that lot.

SUSPENDA   Perhaps you'd show me to his bedroom?

LURCIO   Bedroom?

SUSPENDA   That is why I am here isn't it? To make love all weekend. Every damn sexy gorgeous minute of it.

LURCIO   Well yes . . .

SUSPENDA   Or am I wasting my time? (*She turns to leave.*)

LURCIO   (*blocking her way*) No, no don't go.

SUSPENDA   So where is the bedroom? Or is he going to ravage me here? In full view of the servants?

LURCIO   A free show for us rabble? We should be so
              lucky. (*He opens the bedroom door.*) Please
              wait for my Master in here. This is the
              master bedroom. Where he masters things.
              (*To audience.*) Like how to keep at it for a
              whole weekend!

SUSPENDA   (*stands at the door*) Why don't you bring
              a bottle of your finest wine? To lubricate
              things a little? (*She lets out a cackling laugh
              and exits into the bedroom.*)

LURCIO   (*to audience*) Ye Gods! What a cracker! And
              the Master's going to pull her! He'll be the
              talk of the town at the Roman Legion Club.
              If he's still alive. What a goer! I know what
              you're thinking. You're saying "Yes but is
              Lurcio's poor Master up to it?". Well not
              yet but he soon will be. You see I've got a
              special bottle of love potion under my bed. I
              keep it for special occasions like this and as
              luck would have it I still have a full bottle!
              Anyway, first her wine.

              (*He pops into the cupboard near the steps
              and returns with a bottle of wine. He blows
              some dust off it and gives it a wipe with his
              sleeve.*)

LURCIO   This should do it. (*Reads label.*) It's a very
              good vintage. 11AD. (*Considers this.*) A bit
              like us really. Eleven actors desperate!

              (VOLUPTUA *pops out of the bathroom.*)

VOLUPTUA   Oh Lurky? Come and help me find the soap.
              It keeps slipping about. (*She giggles and
              goes back into the bathroom closing the
              door behind her.*)

LURCIO   Oh dear, I'd forgotten all about her.

                (*He starts to climb the steps. But then*
                SUSPENDA *looks out from the bedroom.*)

SUSPENDA   Where's my drink, slave? I'm parched.
                Bring it to me now! (*She goes back into the
                bedroom closing the door.*)

LURCIO   Oh yes, the wine. (*He turns and heads
                towards the bedroom.*)

VOLUPTUA   (*pops out of the bathroom*) Ready when you
                are Lurcio. (LURCIO *turns around.* VOLUPTUA
                *goes back into the bathroom closing the
                door behind her.*)

SUSPENDA   (*pops out of the bedroom*) I'm getting
                impatient. (LURCIO *turns around again.*
                SUSPENDA *goes back into the bedroom
                closing the door.*)

                (LURCIO *stops and stands in the middle of
                the courtyard. He cannot decide which one
                of the girls to see first.*)

VOLUPTUA   (*at bathroom door*) My hero Lurcio. Come
                and take me . . . (*She goes back into the
                bathroom closing the door.*)

SUSPENDA   (*at bedroom door*) I need something down
                my throat. I'm gasping. Get on with it
                slave!! (*She goes back into the bedroom
                closing the door.*)

                (*Suddenly a third voice joins in.*)

NAUSIUS   (*off*) Lurcio, I want you to drop everything
                and give me one . . .

LURCIO   Eh? I don't remember that one. (*He spins
                around and sees* NAUSIUS *entering through
                the iron gate.*)

NAUSIUS   Lurcio there you are, I want you to drop
                everything and give me one minute of your
                time.

                (LURCIO *is not pleased to see him.*)

LURCIO   What . . .What are you doing back here
                young Master?

NAUSIUS   That beautiful slave girl is not on the ship. I
                have searched everywhere. I've come back
                to seek your advice.

LURCIO   My advice would be to keep looking for her.

NAUSIUS   But where?

LURCIO   Anywhere you like. Just get out there
                and look, young Master. She must be
                somewhere. (*He gently moves* NAUSIUS
                towards the iron gate.)

NAUSIUS   My heart is distraught Lurcio.

LURCIO   (*clutches his chest*) Mine isn't too tip-top
                either. Look why don't you try looking in
                the market.

NAUSIUS   The market?

LURCIO   Down the fruit and veg. She may be hiding
                amongst the melons.

NAUSIUS   It's possible, yes I'll go there.

(*Suddenly a half-naked* SUSPENDA *sticks her head out of the bedroom.*)

SUSPENDA   (*to* LURCIO) Are you going to bring that wine? I'm parched. I like to have a few before I have a few. (*She lets out a cackling laugh and exits into the bedroom.*)

(NAUSIUS *is amazed at what he saw.*)

NAUSIUS   Who . . . Who . . . Who was that Lurcio?

LURCIO   Who was what young Master?

NAUSIUS   That . . . that half-dressed woman in my father's bedroom, that's who.

LURCIO   Oh her.

NAUSIUS   Yes. What's going on here? If you don't tell me straight away Lurcio, I shall have no option but to report all this to my father. On his return from Rome.

LURCIO   Oh don't do that young Master.

NAUSIUS   And I shall tell my mother too.

LURCIO   No! I beg you not to mention it please.

NAUSIUS   Then tell me. Explain the presence of that half-naked woman in there. (*He points at the bedroom.*)

LURCIO   Ah . . .

NAUSIUS   Is she a friend of yours Lurcio?

LURCIO   Well . . . no . . . not exactly. You see I brought her along to . . . to . . . to see you.

NAUSIUS	Me?
LURCIO	Yes.
NAUSIUS	But why should I want to see her Lurcio?
LURCIO	Ah . . . yes . . . well . . . you see that's exactly it. I brought her along so that you could learn about . . . lovemaking.
NAUSIUS	(*excited*) Lovemaking?
LURCIO	Yes, it helps if there are two of you.
NAUSIUS	But this is fantastic news. You mean that she . . . and I . . . you know . . . thingy.
LURCIO	Thingy? I've heard it called some things but never that.
NAUSIUS	We do it together? With each other?
LURCIO	That's the general idea, yes.
NAUSIUS	(*hugs* LURCIO *who tries to push him away*) Oh heavens be praised. I cannot thank you enough Lurcio. (*More hugs which* LURCIO *attempts to resist.*) A beautiful woman just a few feet away from me. You have no idea how I feel at this moment.
LURCIO	You'd be surprised.
NAUSIUS	I'll write her one of my special love odes . . .
LURCIO	She may not want . . .
NAUSIUS	My nib is all a tingle . . .

LURCIO	Yes, well that's the spirit. Just be quick. Tell her who you are but for goodness sake don't mention it to your father. I don't want to get into trouble.

(*Instead of entering the bedroom* NAUSIUS *starts to walk up the steps towards the bathroom.*)

NAUSIUS	I must go and prepare myself.

(LURCIO *runs up the steps and blocks his way.*)

LURCIO	Where are you going? She's waiting in the bedroom for you. Down there. (*He points at bedroom door.*)

NAUSIUS	(*trying to get past* LURCIO) I must present myself looking as clean and tidy as possible.

LURCIO	Believe me she isn't all that fussy.

NAUSIUS	This is an important day Lurcio. One I will remember all my life.

LURCIO	I won't forget it in a hurry either.

NAUSIUS	I must have a wash and brush-up.

LURCIO	You look absolutely fine young Master. As clean as a whistle. You'll be having a dirty time anyway so what's the point?

NAUSIUS	It's a matter of principal.

(*In a final attempt to stop* NAUSIUS *from entering the bathroom,* LURCIO *throws himself against the door.*)

LURCIO	Anyway you can't go in there. I've just remembered there's no water.
NAUSIUS	No water? In the bathroom?
LURCIO	The plumbing's up the creek. I can't get anyone in. They're all on strike.
NAUSIUS	Strike?
LURCIO	Some cash flow problem. They can't get theirs to flow so they're messing up the rest of us.
NAUSIUS	Oh well, I suppose I shall have to forget about a wash and brush-up. (*He starts to walk down the steps.*)
LURCIO	You look fine.
	(*Suddenly* VOLUPTUA *calls from inside the bathroom.*)
VOLUPTUA	(*off*) Yoo-hoo! Are you getting in this bath with me or do you want me to wash myself?
	(NAUSIUS *stops dead in his tracks.*)
NAUSIUS	Who was that?
LURCIO	Who . . . Who was what young Master?
NAUSIUS	That voice?
	(LURCIO, *desperate for an explanation, puts the wine bottle he's carrying to his ear like it's a telephone.*)
LURCIO	(*into bottle*) Hello . . . ? Hello . . . ?

NAUSIUS	It was coming from inside the bathroom. (*He turns around and moves towards the bathroom door.*)
LURCIO	The plumbers must have called off their strike. Changed their tactics.
NAUSIUS	And changed their sex? That was a girl Lurcio.
LURCIO	Well they're not very choosy. As long as you can unblock a sink, you're in.
NAUSIUS	We'll see. (*He pushes past* LURCIO *and looks into the bathroom. He double-takes before finally slamming the door shut.*) That's the slave girl I freed!!
LURCIO	Are you sure?
NAUSIUS	Of course I'm sure. You don't forget a pair like that in a hurry.
LURCIO	Eh? I thought all you saw were her eyes.
NAUSIUS	Exactly. And they were the most beautiful pair of eyes that I have ever set eyes on.
LURCIO	Aye, aye.
NAUSIUS	What I want to know Lurcio is what she is doing in there?
LURCIO	Ah . . . yes . . . well a good question. A very good question.
NAUSIUS	Well? How about a very good answer?

LURCIO	She . . . that is to say I . . . well the thing is . . . (*Inspired.*) I thought I would offer you a choice.
NAUSIUS	A choice?
LURCIO	Between her (*He points at the bathroom.*) and her. (*Points at the bedroom.*)
NAUSIUS	In that case I choose her. (*Points at the bathroom.*)
LURCIO	Yes I thought you might.
NAUSIUS	I must say Lurcio, I'm very grateful to you for going to all this trouble.
LURCIO	Think nothing of it young Master. I had nothing on today. Or at least that was my intention.
	(NAUSIUS *takes a deep breath and is about to enter the bathroom.*)
NAUSIUS	Right, here goes. I've been looking forward to this Lurcio.
LURCIO	I know exactly how you feel.
NAUSIUS	(*suddenly getting cold feet*) But what if I shouldn't . . . you know . . . whatsit . . .
LURCIO	Rise to the occasion?
NAUSIUS	Precisely.
LURCIO	I shouldn't worry young Master. These things have a way of sorting themselves out.
NAUSIUS	I am very nervous, I've got the willies . . .

LURCIO	Look, if you get in there and find it's a bit of a letdown, give me a shout.
NAUSIUS	(*alarmed*) But I don't want you in there Lurcio. Watching!
LURCIO	No, I've got some love potion you see. A nip of that and you'll be up and about in no time.
NAUSIUS	Right, here goes then. (*He opens the bathroom door.*)
LURCIO	Just don't tell your father. Or I'll be BCM!
NAUSIUS	BCM?
LURCIO	Big Cat Meat.
	(*A nervous* NAUSIUS *exits into the bathroom.* LURCIO *turns to the audience.*)
LURCIO	Well what choice did I have? At least he'll enjoy himself once he gets the hang of things.
SUSPENDA	(*looks out from the bedroom*) Where is my wine?? I'm as thirsty as a desert camel who's forgotten to pack its humps! (*Gives a cackling laugh and returns into the bedroom closing the door after her.*)
LURCIO	Oh dear, the laughing hyena! I'd forgotten about her. (*He starts for the bedroom.*)
	(LURCIO *is just about to enter when* LUDICRUS *enters through the iron gate.*)
LUDICRUS	Lurcio! I'm back. Is the coast clear?

LURCIO	Well . . . sort of Master.
LUDICRUS	What? It's Nausius isn't it? What's happened? You're meant to be looking after him. Keeping him away from certain ladies.
LURCIO	Well . . .
LUDICRUS	You have been doing that haven't you Lurcio?
LURCIO	(*glancing at bedroom door*) Well, in a way . . . I suppose. From one anyway.
LUDICRUS	I don't want him hanging around with loose women.
LURCIO	No, Master.
LUDICRUS	So what is he up to?
LURCIO	I'm not entirely sure. Could be anybody's guess.
LUDICRUS	(*lightly*) He's probably somewhere fooling around as usual.
LURCIO	Fooling around . . . yes.
LUDICRUS	Anyway I haven't time to be discussing him, did the beautiful Suspenda get my message?
LURCIO	Yes.
LUDICRUS	Gods be praised!
LURCIO	In fact she's waiting for you in your bedroom now Master.
LUDICRUS	Really?

SUSPENDA	(*off*) Come on Ludicrus, where are you? I'm ready and waiting between your sheets. And I'm getting hot 'n' bothered!!
	(LUDICRUS *goes over to investigate.*)
LUDICRUS	Excellent!
	(*He opens the bedroom door a tiny bit and sees* SUSPENDA *lying on his bed.*)
LUDICRUS	(*licking his lips*) Hmm! Remind me to give you a pay rise Lurcio.
LURCIO	But you don't pay me anything now.
LUDICRUS	In that case I'll double it. This sort of thing mustn't go unrewarded you know.
LURCIO	Just call it devotion beyond the call of duty. (*To audience.*) I sow the oats but he gets 'em!
LUDICRUS	What a wonderful looking woman. (*He shuts the bedroom door.*)
LURCIO	Yes, just don't make her laugh.
LUDICRUS	Good, good. Now I just need a quick wash and brush-up. (*Walks up steps towards the bathroom.*)
LURCIO	(*remembers* NAUSIUS *is in there with* VOLUPTUA) Oh no! (*Rushes ahead of* LUDICRUS.) But you're looking very smart Master. Why keep the lady waiting?
LUDICRUS	I insist on a quick wash and brush-up.
	(SUSPENDA *appears at the bedroom door.*)

SUSPENDA   Ah, there you are. Come on you sexy thing
               Ludicrus. I'm ready, willing and definitely
               able!

LURCIO   A wash and brush-up?

LUDICRUS   (*firmly*) A wash and brush-up.

SUSPENDA   I'm all yours. All yours! (*She goes back into
               the bedroom closing the door.*)

               (*A beat.*)

LURCIO/
LUDICRUS   (*together*) To hell with the wash and brush-
               up!

               (LUDICRUS *races down the steps and goes
               straight into the bedroom. We hear* SUSPENDA
               giving him a warm welcome.)

SUSPENDA   (*off*) There you are you gorgeous man! I
               didn't want to start on my own. (*Gives a
               cackling laugh.*)

LURCIO   He's off! Starter's orders! (*To audience.*) At
               least he didn't find that naive son of his.

               (*A very distraught* NAUSIUS *comes out of the
               bathroom.*)

NAUSIUS   Lurcio! Lurcio!

LURCIO   (*to audience*) Oh dear, here we go. It's the
               excitement of the first time. The thrill of
               it all. The compulsion to brag about it to
               anyone who'll listen. What do you mean you
               can't remember? (*To* NAUSIUS.) How did it
               go young Master? Satisfactory I trust?

NAUSIUS   No Lurcio, it was a total let down.

LURCIO   Don't be too disheartened. If at first you
            don't succeed . . .

NAUSIUS   I couldn't get started Lurcio. I mean I love
            the girl and she seems to like me.

LURCIO   Well that's a good foundation.

NAUSIUS   But for some reason, I couldn't . . . I
            couldn't . . .

LURCIO   Couldn't what young Master? Spit it out?

NAUSIUS   I couldn't . . . (*He whispers in* LURCIO'S *ear.*)

LURCIO   I shall go and get my love potion straight
            away.

NAUSIUS   Would you? Oh thank you Lurcio.

LURCIO   Now you just go back in there and talk
            things over whilst I nip into the house and
            get the bottle.

NAUSIUS   But what shall I talk about?

LURCIO   Anything you like as long as it's not sex.

NAUSIUS   I'll recite one of my love odes.

LURCIO   Tell her about your butterfly collection.

NAUSIUS   Do you think she'll be interested?

LURCIO   No but it's better than having to listen to
            your love odes.

(NAUSIUS *exits into the bathroom.* LURCIO
is about to enter the house when LUDICRUS
*comes running out of the bedroom. His toga
is ripped, laurel crown skew-whiff and he
doesn't look too happy.*)

LURCIO	I trust all is well, Master.
LUDICRUS	No it is not! That woman is a complete nympho, Lurcio!
LURCIO	(*to audience*) Tell me about it. (*To* LUDICRUS.) Really? Lucky old you.
LUDICRUS	She is like a wild cat!
LURCIO	You must control her, Master. Imagine you are Caesar.
LUDICRUS	Forget Caesar, I'll have a seizure! (*He clutches his chest.*)
LURCIO	Oh dear.
LUDICRUS	I'll just collapse in a heap on the floor.
LURCIO	But what a way to go Master.
LUDICRUS	I mean I don't mind a bit of passion. I'm not a prude. Far from it.
LURCIO	But there should be speed limits.
LUDICRUS	Exactly Lurcio. Just where does she get all her sprenergy from?
LURCIO	Sprenergy??
LUDICRUS	(*almost corpsing*) I mean energy. Where does she get all her energy from?

LURCIO	Perhaps she rehearses a lot? (*A beat.*) Unlike us.
LUDICRUS	You'll have to do something Lurcio. Slow down her libido.
LURCIO	(*considers this*) I have the very thing Master. A sleeping potion.
LUDICRUS	(*slightly disappointed*) I don't want her completely knocked out. Just slowed down a bit.
	(SUSPENDA *suddenly comes out of the bedroom and pulls the protesting* LUDICRUS *back into the room.*)
SUSPENDA	Come back you great tower of manhood! (*Gives a cackling laugh.*)
LUDICRUS	(*as he goes*) Be quick Lurcio, be quick! (*He exits.*)
LURCIO	Right, love potion for him (*Pointing at the bathroom.*) and sleeping potion for her (*Pointing at the bedroom.*) It's all go isn't it? (*He exits into the house.*)
	(NAUSIUS, *looking for* LURCIO, *pops his head out of the bathroom.*)
NAUSIUS	Lurcio? Lurcio? Where are you? I need that potion now. She appears not to be interested in my butterfly collection.
VOLUPTUA	(*off*) Who cares about a load of old moths!
NAUSIUS	Hurry! Please! I'm desperate! (*He goes back into the bathroom.*)

(*Suddenly the bedroom door flies open and* LUDICRUS *comes running out hotly pursued by* SUSPENDA.)

LUDICRUS   For goodness sake woman, must we do everything at such a pace!

SUSPENDA   I shall devour you pace by pace! Come here!! (*Gives a cackling laugh.*)

(LUDICRUS *runs around the courtyard chased by* SUSPENDA.)

LUDICRUS   If you would just take things slightly slower.

SUSPENDA   And miss out on all the fun? Never! (*She lets out another cackling laugh.*)

(LURCIO *comes out of the house with his two bottles of potion, identical in shape and size. He watches the two of them circling the courtyard in disbelief.*)

LURCIO   Have I arrived at an inopportune moment Master?

LUDICRUS   Lurcio! She's too much for me! Grab her! She's all yours.

(LURCIO *takes this as an invitation to take* SUSPENDA *off his Master's hands. He doesn't have to be told twice. He waits for the right moment to break into the circle and then starts chasing* SUSPENDA *who is chasing* LUDICRUS. *Round and round they go, in and out of the pillars.*)

LURCIO   I thought you'd never ask Master.

(LUDICRUS *catches up with* LURCIO.)

LUDICRUS	What are you doing man?
LURCIO	Trying to get hold of her. I've always fancied her. Among us slaves she's known as Madeira because she's a piece of . . .
LUDICRUS	Never mind that now!! Have you got the potion?
LURCIO	Yes Master.
LUDICRUS	Well use it, for goodness sake use it!!!

(LURCIO *leaves the circle and leans against a pillar. He is out of breath. He looks at the two bottles.*)

LURCIO	Now which one is which? This one is the love potion and this one is the sleeping potion . . . or is it the other way round?
LUDICRUS	Give her the potion. Now!

(*Just as* LURCIO *is about to act,* SUSPENDA *catches up with* LUDICRUS *and pulls him to the ground. She jumps on top of him and smothers him with kisses.*)

LUDICRUS	(*fighting for breath*) Get on with it Lurcio!!!

(*They roll over so now* LUDICRUS *is on top of* SUSPENDA *and lying between her legs.*)

LURCIO	Are you sure this is the right moment Master?
LUDICRUS	Of course. Get her to swallow it.
LURCIO	But how Master, how?

LUDICRUS   Down her mouth you fool!

LURCIO   (*attempts this*) It's impossible Master. Her
                mouth is full of you!

                (LURCIO *tries to prise them apart but*
                SUSPENDA *pushes her body rhythmically*
                against LUDICRUS.)

LURCIO   (*to audience*) He can't believe his luck! All
                he's ever done are Agatha Christies. You
                don't get that with Miss Marple!

LUDICRUS   You fool Lurcio! You fool! Get it down
                her!!!

LURCIO   (*to* SUSPENDA) Come on, come on, open
                wide! You're good at that!

                (LURCIO *finally manages to pour the potion*
                into SUSPENDA'S *mouth. After a moment's*
                reaction, she passes out with LUDICRUS *lying*
                on top of her.)

LURCIO   Oh!! Thank goodness I didn't give her the
                wrong one. (*To audience.*) You thought
                I was going to didn't you? Admit it. You
                thought old Lurcio's going to cock it up.
                The old mixed-up bottles routine. Ye of
                little faith.

                (*Suddenly* AMMONIA *and* EROTICA *enter*
                through the iron gate. Their baskets can be
                seen in the street behind them. AMMONIA
                can't believe what she sees.)

AMMONIA   Ludicrus!! What are you doing!!!

                (*They all freeze and look at her.*)

LUDICRUS   Ah . . . hello my dear.

AMMONIA   (*furious*) What is the meaning of this???

LUDICRUS   Yes . . . well . . .

(LUDICRUS *climbs off* SUSPENDA'S *body and stands up. He faces* AMMONIA *with his back to the audience and his torn toga falls away completely revealing his bare bottom.*)

AMMONIA   (*horrified*) Ludicrus*!!!*

(LURCIO *quickly covers his Master's shame with the hessian sack.*)

LURCIO   All this fuss over such a small thing.

(*The curtain falls quickly. End of Act One.*)

ACT TWO

Just before the curtain rises SENNA *rushes on and gives us an update in rhyme.*

SENNA

"Woe, woe and thrice woe!
With mighty Vesuvius about to blow,
My predictions came true, my visions not silly.
The one thing we didn't see was the Master's willy!"
Oh nigh, nigh and thrice nigh!

(*She runs off into the wings. The curtain immediately rises and we see everyone as they were at the end of Act One.* LUDICRUS *is now wearing the hessian sack around his middle.*)

AMMONIA

(*furious*) What is going on here?

EROTICA

Daddy, what are you up to?

(LURCIO *quickly runs into the house to find his Master something to wear.*)

LUDICRUS

Well . . . you see . . . er . . . the thing is . . .

AMMONIA

I can see why you wanted us out of the house. I knew you were up to something. That is why I sneaked back.

LUDICRUS

No, you don't understand . . .

(LURCIO *returns from the house with a new toga that* LUDICRUS *quickly puts on.*)

AMMONIA

Very convenient, getting rid of us to your mother Botoxia's.

LUDICRUS

But I can explain . . .

AMMONIA	This I have got to hear.
LURCIO	Me too. (*To audience.*) This should be fun . . . I bet you're glad you came back after the interval now.
	(EROTICA *gets ready to write it all down on her slate.*)
LUDICRUS	This is not what you think it is.
EROTICA	(*looking at* SUSPENDA'S *body*) Is she dead, daddy? (*During the following* EROTICA *busily writes down all the events on her slate like a court recorder.*)
LUDICRUS	What? No, no . . .
AMMONIA	Why were you lying on top of her?
LUDICRUS	Well I . . . I . . .
LURCIO	(*quickly stepping in*) The Master was reviving her, Mistress.
AMMONIA	Reviving her?
LURCIO	Yes the poor lady fainted.
AMMONIA	Fainted?
LUDICRUS	(*sotto*) Brilliant! (*To* AMMONIA.) That's right, she fainted. Right in front of us. Toppled over.
LURCIO	And she's got a lot to topple!
AMMONIA	I see.
LURCIO	She hadn't eaten anything you see.

LUDICRUS   Nothing. Not a bite.

                 (EROTICA *is still chalking it all up on her slate.*)

AMMONIA   But who is this woman, Ludicrus?

LUDICRUS   Yes well . . . there is a very simple explanation my dear.

AMMONIA   What is it then?

LUDICRUS   Well . . . first of all this woman is not interested in me.

LURCIO   In her state she's not interested in anyone!

AMMONIA   Then what is she doing here lying half-naked in my courtyard? Toppling over from lack of food?

LUDICRUS   This woman isn't interested in me, she's interested in . . . Lurcio.

AMMONIA   What??

EROTICA   What?

LURCIO   What?? (*To audience.*) Drop me in it why don't you?

AMMONIA   (*incredulous*) Lurcio?

EROTICA   Lurcio? Urgh! Gross! (*Starts writing madly away on her slate.*)

LUDICRUS   Yes.

AMMONIA   Don't be ridiculous. No girl would be interested in Lurcio.

EROTICA   Absolutely not! Lurcio? Urgh!!

LUDICRUS   Well I follow your point dear but . . .

LURCIO   (*sotto*) Charming. (*He looks hurt.*)

LUDICRUS   The . . . the thing is I unexpectedly had
             to return from my trip and I found Lurcio
             cavorting with that woman. Didn't I Lurcio?
             (*He winks heavily at* LURCIO.)

LURCIO   What? Oh yes, Master. (*To audience.*)
             Cavorting? Chance would be a fine thing.
             Didn't get near a cavort.

LUDICRUS   And then she suddenly fainted.

AMMONIA   I'm not surprised, cavorting with him.
             Lurcio! Come here!

             (LURCIO *stands between* LUDICRUS *and*
             AMMONIA.)

LURCIO   Yes Mistress.

AMMONIA   Did you bring that awful woman into our
             house?

             (LURCIO *puts out his hand indicating that*
             LUDICRUS *must put money in it so that he*
             won't spill the beans. AMMONIA *does not see*
             this.)

LURCIO   I did Mistress. (LUDICRUS *puts some coins*
             into LURCIO's *hand.*)

AMMONIA   So she has nothing whatever to do with my
             husband? (LURCIO *signals for more money.*
             LUDICRUS *pays up.*)

LURCIO   Absolutely not, Mistress.

AMMONIA   You would swear on your life about this
                would you? (LURCIO *again puts his hand out
                and once again* LUDICRUS *pays up.*)

LURCIO   I would swear on my miserable life Mistress
                that the Master had nothing to do with that
                woman coming to this house. She was all
                my doing. (*To audience.*) And very little
                undoing.

AMMONIA   Really? Well Lurcio, you've let me down
                again. I see I shall have to reconsider your
                position in this house.

LURCIO   But Mistress . . .

AMMONIA   I shall speak to you later. And to think I
                accused my poor husband of cheating on
                me.

LURCIO   Oh, he would never do that.

AMMONIA   Not with me as his wife he wouldn't. Why
                go out for a pizza when you've got a hog's
                head at home?

LURCIO   Hmm . . .

AMMONIA   Come on Erotica. (*She heads for the house
                swiftly followed by* EROTICA.) And will you
                put that slate down!

EROTICA   (*as she goes*) Forget slating, I'm going to
                write a best-selling scroll! (*Holds up her
                slate.*)

                (*They both exit into the house.*)

LUDICRUS   Well done Lurcio. I shall not forget this.

LURCIO   Neither shall I.

LUDICRUS   That was a close one. I only got out of it
            by . . .

LURCIO   Lying?

LUDICRUS   . . . the skin of my teeth. Now we must get
            rid of that woman Suspenda before she
            wakes up and tells my wife the truth. If
            Ammonia finds that I sent that note inviting
            her round, I'm dead.

LURCIO   Right. I'll have to carry her body back to
            her villa.

LUDICRUS   No that's too risky. We must get her out of
            the picture for a while.

LURCIO   (*horrified*) What? Kill her??

LUDICRUS   No, no. What about that slave galley ship in
            the docks?

LURCIO   The one owned by Captain Treacherus?

LUDICRUS   That's the one. Go to the docks and tell him
            one of his slaves is here. Persuade him to
            take her away. By the time the mistake is
            sorted out, Ammonia will have forgotten all
            about this business. Now first help me hide
            her.

            (*Between them they lift* SUSPENDA *up.* LURCIO
            picks her up under her arms and LUDICRUS
            grabs her legs.)

LURCIO   But where shall we put her?

LUDICRUS   In the bathroom.

LURCIO   Good idea. (*They carry* SUSPENDA *to the
            bottom of the steps.* LURCIO *suddenly
            remembers* NAUSIUS *is in there.*) No! No,
            we'll never get her up the steps Master.

LUDICRUS   What about the well?

LURCIO   The well? Yes . . .

            (*They carry* SUSPENDA *over to the well.*
            LUDICRUS *looks down the shaft.*)

LUDICRUS   It's very deep.

            (LURCIO *looks down the well too.*)

LURCIO   I've heard of pussy in the well but this is
            ridiculous. If we drop her in there we'll
            never get her out again.

LUDICRUS   Where then?

            (*They look for another place to hide her.*)

LURCIO   How about the cupboard, Master?

LUDICRUS   Good idea.

            (*They carry* SUSPENDA *into the cupboard
            under the steps, closing the door behind
            them. An anxious* NAUSIUS *looks out from the
            bathroom.*)

NAUSIUS   (*desperate*) Lurcio? Where's that blasted
            love potion?

            (VOLUPTUA *appears behind him.*)

VOLUPTUA	Who are you talking to?
NAUSIUS	My slave, he's er . . . promised me something.
VOLUPTUA	I know the feeling.
NAUSIUS	Perhaps if I was to tell you more about my butterfly collection?
VOLUPTUA	(*fed up*) I'd rather be doing something else, Nausius.
NAUSIUS	(*desperate*) Well so would I!!
	(*They exit back into the bathroom.* LURCIO *comes out of the cupboard on his own.*)
LUDICRUS	(*off*) I'll keep an eye on her, Lurcio. You get down to the docks.
LURCIO	(*to audience*) Oh dear! Now what? If I go to the docks and that Captain Treacherus sees me again he'll throw me in chains and put me on the Mediterranean cruise with no sun. What I need is a miracle.
	(CORNEOUS *enters through the iron gate carrying the crate* LURCIO *gave him earlier.*)
LURCIO	(*with eyes to heaven*) Thank you. (*To* CORNEOUS.) You're back then?
CORNEOUS	Yes, got a little held-up.
LURCIO	From what I heard it was the wall that needed holding up.
CORNEOUS	Eh?

Lurcio	Oh never mind. The Master's got a job for you.
Corneous	(*keenly*) The Master? How did it go?
Lurcio	Never you mind, he's asked for you personally to run an errand for him.
Corneous	He can rely on me.
Lurcio	He wants you to go down to the docks and find Captain Treacherus.
Corneous	Captain Treacherus? *The* Captain Treacherus?
Lurcio	Yes, I thought that would shake you up a bit.
Corneous	What do I do when I find him?
Lurcio	You're to tell him that an escaped slave girl from his galley is hiding in this house.
Corneous	And is there a girl hiding in this house?
Lurcio	Listen mate, every girl in Pompeii is hiding in there at the moment – believe me.
Corneous	Really? (*He's tries to get a look through the windows.*)
Lurcio	Look, get down to the docks and do your job. Leave the lusting to me. It's written into my contract. I call it my shopping lust! (*To audience.*) Get it? Shopping lust. Oh please yourselves . . .
Corneous	Right. (*He exits through the gate.*)

LURCIO	There he goes. And with any luck he'll deliver the message and then get press-ganged into being a galley slave. Now what was I doing?
	(NAUSIUS *and* VOLUPTUA *can be heard in the bathroom.*)
VOLUPTUA	(*off*) But Nausius why is it so small?? I can hardly see it! It's tiny!!
NAUSIUS	(*off*) What? Well . . . that particular species has a small wing span.
VOLUPTUA	(*off*) I wasn't referring to your bloomin' butterfly!!
	(*A beat.*)
LURCIO	Oh yes, the love potion. (*He starts to climb the steps to the bathroom.*)
	(*There is a loud volcanic roar off.* LURCIO *looks into the wings to investigate.*)
LURCIO	Oh here we go, old Vesuvius is off again!
	(*There is a loud thunder flash and smoke and* SENNA *suddenly enters through the iron gate, wailing.* LURCIO *leaps back in horror.*)
SENNA	Nigh, nigh and thrice nigh!
LURCIO	Oh for goodness sake!! Not now!
SENNA	I must warn you of dark happenings.
LURCIO	Look, I haven't the time for this. Go away.

SENNA   You are going on a journey. I see a dark
               place, black as night.

LURCIO   You'll have to leave . . .

SENNA   It is cold and damp.

LURCIO   Out!

SENNA   Woe, woe and thrice woe!

LURCIO   Go, go and thrice go! (*He pushes her into
               the stable and locks the doors after her.*)
               You'll find it cold and damp in there. Silly
               old bag. Now where was I? Oh yes the
               young Master . . .

               (LURCIO *is about to enter the bathroom when*
               AMMONIA *comes out of the house. She is
               carrying two empty green wine bottles and a
               small saw.*)

AMMONIA   Lurcio, I think you and I should have those
               words.

LURCIO   Could we not have words later, Mistress?

AMMONIA   No we could not. What on earth has got in
               to you today? I don't employ you to invite
               strange women to this house to ogle.

LURCIO   Ogle? Chance would be a fine thing.

AMMONIA   Anyway, I want you to cut off the ends of
               these bottles and make me some goggles for
               swimming. (LURCIO *reacts.*)

               (*She hands the bottles and saw to* LURCIO.
               During the following conversation he

removes the base of each bottle. (*NB: These are prop bottles with detachable bases.*)

LURCIO   (*baffled*) Goggles for swimming, Mistress?

AMMONIA   Yes. You're always saying how good you are with your hands. (*She sits down on the stone. He sits beside her.*)

LURCIO   (*starts sawing first bottle*) Goggles coming up then. (*The bottle base immediately drops off. An amazed* LURCIO *looks at it on the ground.*) I must have a natural gift for this.

AMMONIA   I am getting rather fed up with your cheek, Lurcio. Remember that you are a servant. I don't want you asking strange weird women to my home. (*A beat.*) Find one already here.

             (LURCIO *reacts.*)

AMMONIA   What I mean is, have you considered Cook?

LURCIO   (*horrified*) Cook??

AMMONIA   They say she has lovely eyes.

LURCIO   Yes when she can focus.

AMMONIA   And lovely hair.

LURCIO   Those rat-tails?

AMMONIA   And lovely hands.

LURCIO   Yes, if you could only get her to let go of the bottle what a peach she'd be.

AMMONIA   Well take it or leave it Lurcio . . .

LURCIO	I'll leave it if it's all the same.
AMMONIA	I mean, don't think me unreasonable. Far from it. Naturally we all have needs. I know that I do.
LURCIO	I have heard this. (*To audience.*) Her nickname is "Eclipse" – everyone has seen it at one time or another! (*To* AMMONIA.) You were saying Mistress?
AMMONIA	Well . . . (*She points to his saw.*) Will you saw off another goggle . . .
LURCIO	Oh yes . . .
	(*He starts sawing the second bottle and, again, the base immediately drops off and falls to the ground.* LURCIO *feels a small sense of triumph.*)
LURCIO	(*to audience*) I could make a living at this.
AMMONIA	Only yesterday something wonderful happened at the public baths.
LURCIO	At the baths?
AMMONIA	I was busy minding my own business when I suddenly heard this voice through the steam. I couldn't place it at first but then I suddenly remembered who it was.
LURCIO	And who was it Mistress?
AMMONIA	It was the man who taught me to swim when I was Erotica's age.
LURCIO	Indeed?

AMMONIA   I immediately jumped into the water but in
                 all the steam he just brushed past me.

LURCIO   Oh dear.

AMMONIA   By the time it had cleared he had gone.
                 But I know it was him. (*A beat.*) You don't
                 forget a breast-stroke like that in a hurry.

LURCIO   No . . .

AMMONIA   (*dreamily*) I just hope that I bump into him
                 again. He was a wonderful man.

                 (LURCIO *hands the two bottle bases to*
                 AMMONIA. *She holds them up to her eyes.*)

AMMONIA   Now I've got some goggles, I'll be ready
                 for him. Show him a few of my latest
                 techniques.

                 (AMMONIA *exits into the house.*)

LURCIO   Hmm . . .

                 (*Suddenly* CORNEOUS *comes running through
                 the gate. He is out of breath.*)

CORNEOUS   Quick! Hide me!

LURCIO   What's happened?

CORNEOUS   I bumped into that Captain Treacherus down
                 at the docks.

LURCIO   Yeesss . . .

CORNEOUS   And I told him that escaped slave girl was
                 hiding here.

LURCIO   Good, he can take her away.

CORNEOUS   But he took one look at me and then he said
                he wanted to chain my feet up.

LURCIO   (*enjoying it*) Did he?

CORNEOUS   He wants to send me on a Mediterranean
                cruise with no sun.

LURCIO   I see, well maybe you would enjoy it. You
                know, you and your feet . . .

CORNEOUS   But there is worse; he's going to have the
                Master arrested for hiding her in the first
                place.

LURCIO   (*horrified*) What??

CORNEOUS   Why would the Master do such a thing?

LURCIO   He didn't, I did. Treacherus came by here
                earlier.

CORNEOUS   You hid the slave girl? Why?

LURCIO   Because she promised me . . . (*Confusing
                himself.*) . . . no that was the other slave girl
                . . . hang on there's only one slave girl . . . oh
                look it's a long story.

CORNEOUS   Then as soon as this Captain Treacherus
                discovers that the Master had nothing to do
                with hiding the slave girl, we're both for it.

LURCIO   Not if we think quickly.

CORNEOUS   What do you mean?

LURCIO   Well Captain Treacherus is on his way here
                 looking for you and me, right?

CORNEOUS   That's right, he's seen both our faces.
                 (*Terrified.*) I don't want to be strapped to an
                 oar.

LURCIO   Yes, yes we've done that gag. In Act One.
                 Died a death then too. Look, I've just had an
                 idea . . .

                 (*He grabs a couple of* AMMONIA'S *baskets
                 and then with* CORNEOUS *exits into the house.
                 There is a loud banging from* SENNA *on the
                 stable doors.*)

SENNA   (*off*) Let me out! Let me out! I don't
                 like it in here. Woe, woe and thrice woe!
                 (*She hears no response.*) Woe, woe! (*No
                 response.*) Woe! (*A beat.*) I suppose I could
                 pass the time by rubbing my balls . . .

                 (LUDICRUS *cautiously comes out of the
                 cupboard looking for* LURCIO.)

LUDICRUS   Lurcio? Where are you? Have you been
                 down to the docks?

                 (NAUSIUS *comes out of the bathroom.*)

NAUSIUS   Lurcio? Have you got the potion?

                 (*They suddenly see each other. They smile
                 politely.*)

NAUSIUS   Ah, Pater.

LUDICRUS   Nausius my boy.

NAUSIUS   Are you well today?

LUDICRUS   I'm fine. You?

NAUSIUS   Well you know, so-so.

LUDICRUS   This and that?

NAUSIUS   Up and . . . down. (*He reacts to what he has said.*)

LUDICRUS   Lurcio mentioned that you were around. I suggested that he talked to you about hobbies and things.

NAUSIUS   Hobbies?

LUDICRUS   I was always impressed with your butterfly collection.

NAUSIUS   (*with an eye on the bathroom door*) I wish others were as keen.

LUDICRUS   Anyway, I'm sure Lurcio will get you interested in something.

NAUSIUS   Oh yes, I'm sure he will. What are you doing here anyway, Pater? I thought you were going to Rome.

LUDICRUS   Me? Oh nothing in particular. I got my dates mixed up. My bill in the Senate is next week.

NAUSIUS   I see.

                (*There's a pause. Each of them wishes the other would be on their way.*)

LUDICRUS   Well I suppose I'd better be moving on.

NAUSIUS   Yes, me too.

LUDICRUS	Were you doing anything in particular here today?
NAUSIUS	Me? No, nothing in particular.
LUDICRUS	Hmm . . .
NAUSIUS	Hmm . . .
LUDICRUS	Seems to be a very popular pastime around here today. Anyway, I was just popping into the bathroom for a wash and brush-up.
	(LUDICRUS *heads for the bathroom.* NAUSIUS *gets there first and blocks his way.*)
NAUSIUS	Sorry Pater, I was just about to bathe.
LUDICRUS	You were about to bathe?
NAUSIUS	Yes. I want to take all my clothes off and jump in. (*A beat.*) If you see Lurcio, send him in won't you? He's going to slip me a little something. (*He quickly exits into the bathroom.*)
LUDICRUS	Strange boy.
	(SUSPENDA, *in the cupboard, can be heard moaning and groaning.*)
SUSPENDA	(*off*) Ludicrus?? Where are you? It's as dark as Hades in here! Hells bells!! (*She lets out a cackling laugh.*)
LUDICRUS	Oh no! She's coming round. She needs more sleeping potion.
	(*He grabs the bottle of sleeping potion and exits into the cupboard. There is a lot of*

shouting and noise off and then CAPTAIN
TREACHERUS *and* KRETINUS *enter through the
gate.*)

TREACHERUS   This is the house Kretinus. The one where
that slave said the escaped slave girl is
hiding.

KRETINUS   (*looking around*) There's no one around.

TREACHERUS   We must first find that Ludicrus Sextus. I
knew he was up to no good. They're all the
same these Senators. Hypocrites! They say
one thing but pull another . . .

KRETINUS   Right. (*Looking around.*) I can't see him.

TREACHERUS   Of course you can't you numbskull – he's
hiding! He knows the penalty for helping
escaped slaves. What we have to do is flush
him out.

KRETINUS   He could be anywhere. Anywhere.

TREACHERUS   It's good to see, Kretinus, that when the
Gods were handing out the brains they
didn't overlook you. Of course he could
be anywhere. The question is where? (*He
approaches the house.*) Let's start in here.

(TREACHERUS *is about to enter when* LURCIO
and CORNEOUS *now dressed as women
in* AMMONIA'S *clothes/wigs come out of
the house. They speak in high-pitched
effeminate voices.*)

LURCIO   Oh hello! The boys are here.

CORNEOUS   Super!

LURCIO   Us ladies always like a man in uniform.

CORNEOUS   Oh yes, I do so love a man with a lengthy
                scabbard.

LURCIO   (*cautiously*) Well yes, so do I. As long as he
                keeps his weapon tucked inside it.

TREACHERUS   Who are you?

CORNEOUS   Well I am Corneous . . . Cornia . . . Pornia.

TREACHERUS   Cornia-Pornia?

CORNEOUS   C.P. for short. And this is my sister . . .
                Ammonia.

LURCIO   Yes I'm . . . (*Horrified.*) Ammonia!!!!

CORNEOUS   The wife of Ludicrus Sextus who isn't here
                at the moment.

TREACHERUS   That is a shame as I wished to see him. (*All
                charm.*) Anyway I am pleased to meet you
                ladies.

KRETINUS   And so am I. My name is Kretinus. (*He
                steps forward to kiss* LURCIO'S *hand but*
                TREACHERUS *stops him with his sword.*)

TREACHERUS   Yes, shut up Kretinus, no one's interested.
                (*To* LURCIO.) I am Captain Treacherus.
                Perhaps you've heard of me?

LURCIO   No I don't think so. Are you one of the
                Florence Treacheruses? They're an arty lot.
                (*He looks at* TREACHERUS.) No probably not.

TREACHERUS   No.

LURCIO

Or the Rome Treacheruses? They always say
a Roman Treacherus is highly intelligent.
(*Looks at* TREACHERUS *doubtfully.*) Yes,
well . . .

TREACHERUS

No, I am from Naples.

LURCIO

I can't remember what they say about the
Naples Treacheruses.

TREACHERUS

I can. It's, "a Naples Treacherus is very
lecherous". (*He moves close to* LURCIO.)

LURCIO

(*steps back in horror*) Yes, well I have never
been there.

CORNEOUS

Yes you have Ammonia. We went there on
our holidays last year.

LURCIO

Did we C.P.?

CORNEOUS

(*enjoying it*) Yes you remember. You met
that dashing engineer who showed you his
aqueducts. (LURCIO *reacts.*)

LURCIO

(*sotto*) Don't push it!!

TREACHERUS

The thing is we are here looking for your
husband. Apparently he's been hiding a
slave girl in this house.

CORNEOUS

Surely not!

LURCIO

Impossible.

CORNEOUS

Ludie hiding?

LURCIO

Highly unludie!

TREACHERUS   Yes, we were tipped off by a runt of a slave that we should come here.

LURCIO   How interesting. A runt of a slave you say?

TREACHERUS   Yes, odious man. Enormous feet.

CORNEOUS   (*sotto to* LURCIO) I should deck him!

LURCIO   (*sotto to* CORNEOUS) Steady or we're both going to end up in the galley.

TREACHERUS   Have either of you ladies seen the Senator?

CORNEOUS   Oh no.

LURCIO   Not a squeak.

CORNEOUS   Or a peep.

LURCIO   Or a peep-squeak.

TREACHERUS   I need to speak to him. It is a serious matter hiding slaves. Perhaps if we were to look in the house? (*He starts for the house.*)

LURCIO   (*blocking the way*) No, there's nobody in there.

CORNEOUS   Nobody.

LURCIO   A waste of your time.

CORNEOUS   Total time-waste.

LURCIO   Waste of space.

TREACHERUS   You're sure?

CORNEOUS   Quite sure.

LURCIO   Certain.

CORNEOUS   Absolutely.

LURCIO   Absolutely certified.

TREACHERUS   (*circling* LURCIO) You know, I'm sure I've
                seen you somewhere before.

LURCIO   I don't think so.

TREACHERUS   I never forget a face.

LURCIO   Not mine.

TREACHERUS   Maybe down at the baths?

LURCIO   No, I don't like bathing.

TREACHERUS   Or at the chariot races?

LURCIO   No, I don't like chariots.

TREACHERUS   Or at the cock fighting dens?

LURCIO   No, I don't like . . . Look I think you must
                have muddled me up with someone else.

TREACHERUS   Possible I suppose. (*He pinches* LURCIO'S
                behind.)

LURCIO   Oi!!! Watch it mush!

TREACHERUS   A lady of spirit? I like that in a woman.

KRETINUS   So do I Treacherus. That and a flagon of
                wine. That way they can't see how stupid I am.

TREACHERUS   Imbecile! (*To* LURCIO.) Perhaps you would
                like to accompany me on my next voyage?

We could head out to sea together. You
could adorn my cabin.

LURCIO   No thanks. I'm prone to sea-sickness. As
soon as I leave port I start throwing up.

TREACHERUS   Buckets?

LURCIO   No it's true.

TREACHERUS   No, buckets. I could have buckets placed
around the cabin until you're better.

                (*Suddenly* LUDICRUS *enters backwards from
                inside the cupboard dragging the drugged
                body of* SUSPENDA.)

TREACHERUS   And who have we here?

LURCIO   (*quickly*) This is my slave Lurcio. (LUDICRUS
                reacts and recognises LURCIO.)

LUDICRUS   (*sotto to* LURCIO) Lurcio? What on earth??

LURCIO   (*sotto to* LUDICRUS) Ssshhh!!!

TREACHERUS   Is he a licensed slave, Ammonia?

LURCIO   Oh yes. The Captain here was just saying
                that the penalty for hiding slaves is severe.
                Very severe.

LUDICRUS   What?

CORNEOUS   And that your Master will be in a lot
                of bother when the Captain catches up
                with him. Wasn't that your gist, Captain
                Treacherus?

                (LUDICRUS *now recognises* CORNEOUS.)

LUDICRUS   (*sotto*) Corneous??

CORNEOUS   (*sotto to* LUDICRUS) Ssshh Master!!

TREACHERUS   Oh yes. I shall take pleasure in turning him
                in personally.

LURCIO   (*to* LUDICRUS) So your Master better be very
                careful if he knows what's good for him.

LUDICRUS   (*catching on*) Oh yes . . . Mistress.

TREACHERUS   And who is this? (*He points at* SUSPENDA.)

LUDICRUS   Ah this is . . . is . . .

CORNEOUS   This must be the slave girl you were looking
                for.

TREACHERUS   She doesn't say much does she?

CORNEOUS   No, she's very tired.

LUDICRUS   Very tired.

LURCIO   Knackered!

TREACHERUS   (*investigating*) Are you sure this is the slave
                girl? I'm not sure she's going to be much
                good to me in that state.

LUDICRUS   I'm sure she'll perk up when she's chained
                up on your galley.

                (TREACHERUS *is surprised by* LUDICRUS'S
                opinion.)

TREACHERUS   Excuse me but do you mind keeping your
                nose out of it – slave!

LURCIO	Yes Lurcio, sweep the courtyard or something.
	(*A reluctant* LUDICRUS *picks up a broom and starts sweeping.*)
TREACHERUS	Now what this slave girl needs is a bit of picking up.
LURCIO	(*sotto*) She's pretty good at that, trust me.
TREACHERUS	A bit of refreshment. (*Sees bottle of love potion.*) Now what's this?
LURCIO	No!!
LUDICRUS	That won't refresh her. (*Shakes his head.*) Not a chance.
	(TREACHERUS *reacts to this.*)
TREACHERUS	Will you shut up slave! This is none of your business.
	(LUDICRUS *returns to his sweeping.*)
LURCIO	Perhaps Lurcio was out of place to say it but I feel he may have a point. I don't think you should give the slave girl that bottle.
TREACHERUS	Why ever not?
LURCIO	Because you don't know what's inside it.
TREACHERUS	(*sniffing bottle*) It smells all right.
LURCIO	Yes but will it taste all right?
TREACHERUS	There's one way to find out. (*He hands bottle to* LUDICRUS.) Slave, take a sip of this.

LUDICRUS   No!

TREACHERUS   What did you say slave? Drink it!

LUDICRUS   (*can pretend no more*) I will not! Now listen
                to me Captain whatever-your-name-is,
                there's something you should know . . .

LURCIO   Shut up Lurcio!!!

CORNEOUS   Yes, shut up Lurcio!!!

TREACHERUS   (*to* LUDICRUS) You insubordinate slave,
                you'll do as you're told. (*He holds his sword
                to* LUDICRUS's *throat.*) If I asked Kretinus
                to drink from the bottle, he would obey me
                instantly.

KRETINUS   Of course I would.

                (*Suddenly* KRETINUS *grabs the bottle.*)

TREACHERUS   What are you doing you imbecile!!

                (*Before* TREACHERUS *can stop him,* KRETINUS
                *takes a sip from the bottle and starts
                reacting in a strange way. He rolls his eyes,
                makes funny noises and looks around him
                in a lustful way as the love potion takes full
                effect.*)

TREACHERUS   What on earth's got into you, Kretinus??

KRETINUS   I feel very strange. (*Approaches* LURCIO.)
                Whamus, bamus, thank you ma'mus! Let's
                get at it! Let's get at it!

LURCIO   (*moving away*) Well not with me you don't!
                Push off!!

KRETINUS   Come here my darling and give me a
                  smacker on the lips!!

LURCIO   What???

                  (KRETINUS *chases* LURCIO *around the
                  courtyard and into the house.* CORNEOUS *and*
                  LUDICRUS *follow to try and rescue* LURCIO.)

CORNEOUS   (*as he goes*) Wait! Come back!

LUDICRUS   (*as he goes*) Yes . . . er Mistress, come back!

TREACHERUS   I knew promoting that Kretinus was a
                  mistake. (*He looks at* SUSPENDA.) Are you
                  sure you're one of my slaves? I'm sure
                  I would have remembered you. (*He tries
                  to wake her up by shaking her.*) Wake up!
                  Wake up! (*He gives up.*) You're not going to
                  be any good on my galley. (*He sits down on
                  stone.*) What I need is someone who can roll
                  my rowlocks!

                  (AMMONIA'S *silhouette appears at a
                  window.*)

AMMONIA   I'm here! I recognise that voice. It is the
                  one I have been waiting for. (*Calls out.*)
                  Oh Captain Treachywetchy? Captain
                  Treachywetchy?

TREACHERUS   Who calls my name?

AMMONIA   It is I, your water baby. I have waited long
                  for this moment. To be reunited with you my
                  darling Captain Treachywetchy.

TREACHERUS   That voice? It sounds familiar. What is your
                  name?

AMMONIA   Surely you haven't forgotten? It is I,
                 Ammonia. (TREACHERUS *reacts*.) We brushed
                 past each other earlier, don't say it didn't
                 mean anything to you?

TREACHERUS   But . . . but I thought you weren't interested.

AMMONIA   Oh I was just playing for time. I had to be
                 sure you felt the same.

TREACHERUS   So you would be happy to come to sea with
                 me after all?

AMMONIA   The sea, the lake, the baths. Whatever takes
                 your fancy.

TREACHERUS   I thought you didn't like the baths.

AMMONIA   Oh they're all right. As long as it's not too
                 steamy. I hate it when there are too many
                 bodies going up and down, up and down.

TREACHERUS   I see.

AMMONIA   Much better when there's only two of us
                 going up and down. (TREACHERUS *reacts*.)

TREACHERUS   Er . . . yes.

AMMONIA   In perfect synchronisation of course.

TREACHERUS   Of course . . . and what else did you have in
                 mind exactly, Ammonia?

AMMONIA   Well, I thought maybe you could show me
                 some of your strokes.

TREACHERUS   My strokes??

AMMONIA   And if you're very good I'll let you muck
                 around with my goggles.

TREACHERUS   (*can't believe his ears*) Indeed.

AMMONIA   Now don't go away, I'll just get ready and
                 me and my goggles will come and join you.
                 (*She exits from the window.*)

TREACHERUS   This must be my lucky day!!

                 (SENNA *can be heard groaning from inside
                 the stable.*)

SENNA   (*off*) Woe, woe and thrice woe!

                 (*An inquisitive* TREACHERUS *draws his
                 sword and crosses to the stable doors to
                 investigate.*)

TREACHERUS   Who's in there??

                 (*More groaning is heard followed by . . .*)

SENNA   (*off*) Nay, nay and thrice nay!

TREACHERUS   (*satisfied*) Ah, it is only a horse. (*He walks
                 away.*)

                 (*An out-of-breath* LURCIO *comes running out
                 of the house still being chased by* KRETINUS.
                 They are immediately followed by CORNEOUS
                 and LUDICRUS.*)

LURCIO   (*to* KRETINUS) Will you leave me alone!!!

TREACHERUS   (*to* LURCIO) Ah! There you are my dear
                 Ammonia.

LURCIO   Yes, please call off this idiot!

TREACHERUS   I'm afraid it's your allure my dear.

LURCIO   What??

TREACHERUS   You are attracting men like flies today.

LURCIO   Yes well swat off!!

TREACHERUS   And I for one am completely under your
              spell. I love it when you call me Captain
              Treachywetchy.

LURCIO   Captain Treachywetchy???

TREACHERUS   Now let's get down to my ship and spend
              some time down below.

LURCIO   Down below?

TREACHERUS   Just the two of us.

LURCIO   What?? Have you gone mad? I want nothing
              to do with you or your ship.

TREACHERUS   But you said you wanted to see my strokes.

LURCIO   (*horrified*) What???

TREACHERUS   And if I was good, you'd let me muck
              around with your goggles!

              (KRETINUS *tries to embrace* LURCIO.)

LURCIO   (*to* KRETINUS) Will you leave me alone!!!

TREACHERUS   Yes, leave the woman alone Kretinus. She is
              spoken for. She is mine, not yours. (*Shouts.*)
              Do I make myself clear you moron! Two's
              company but three's a crowd.

(This stops Kretinus. *His lustful eyes now turn to* Treacherus.)

KRETINUS   Oh, Mr Bossy Boots, eh?

TREACHERUS   What?

KRETINUS   I like a man in charge.

TREACHERUS   Have you taken leave of your senses??

KRETINUS   We can have an orgy, just the three of us!

TREACHERUS   An orgy???

KRETINUS   Two's company but three's allowed. That's what you said.

TREACHERUS   I said a crowd you idiot! Three's a crowd.

KRETINUS   Come here!! Get your kit off!!

TREACHERUS   Have you gone mad you crazy buffoon? Keep away!!! I'm not having an orgy with you!!

              *(*Kretinus *chases* Treacherus *around the courtyard.* Suspenda *wakes up and surveys the scene.)*

SUSPENDA   An orgy!! Did someone mention an orgy? About bloody time! *(Her attention turns to* Ludicrus.*)* Now where were we before we were so rudely interrupted?

              (She jumps on top of Ludicrus *and smothers him in kisses.)*

LUDICRUS   Aaahhh!!! Get off woman! Get off!!!

(EROTICA *enters from house. She approaches* CORNEOUS.)

EROTICA   Excuse me madam but have you seen . . .
                 (*Recognising* CORNEOUS.) Brilliant disguise
                 Corneous! Mummy will never find out!

                 (EROTICA *and* CORNEOUS *embrace.* KRETINUS
                 then chases TREACHERUS *towards the iron*
                 gate.)

KRETINUS   Come here orgy master!!

TREACHERUS   You will pay for this Kretinus you imbecile!
                 I will thrash you to within an inch of your
                 pathetic life!!

KRETINUS   I love it when you talk dirty!

                 (*They quickly exit. Suddenly* NAUSIUS *comes*
                 out of the bathroom looking for LURCIO.
                 VOLUPTUA, *wearing only a towel, follows*
                 him.)

VOLUPTUA   Where are you going?

NAUSIUS   I've got to find my servant. Lurcio? Lurcio?
                 Where is that potion?

                 (LURCIO, *forgetting that he is dressed as a*
                 woman, crosses to NAUSIUS.)

LURCIO   It's all gone young Master but if I can help
                 in any other way, I'm all yours.

NAUSIUS   And who are you madam? (*Recognising*
                 LURCIO.) Aaahhh!! Lurcio!! (*He turns and*
                 bumps straight into VOLUPTUA *standing*
                 behind him.)

VOLUPTUA	(*enjoying the physical contact*) Ooohh!! I wish you'd make up your mind Nausius. Are you coming or going?
	(*They embrace and her towel falls away. It lands on something sticking out of* NAUSIUS *halfway down his body.*)
LURCIO	I think we know the answer to that one.
	(AMMONIA *suddenly enters from the house. She is dressed to go swimming wearing only a bathing robe and her green goggles.*)
AMMONIA	Are you ready Captain Treachywetchy? (*She removes her goggles and surveys the scene.*) What the hell is going on?????
	(*Everyone freezes in their compromising positions.* LURCIO *and* CORNEOUS *quickly take off their wigs.*)
LURCIO	Oh dear! Here we go. (*To audience.*) The traditional "uh-oh" moment!
AMMONIA	Ludicrus!!!
LUDICRUS	Ammonia??
AMMONIA	Nausius??
NAUSIUS	Mater!!
AMMONIA	Erotica??
EROTICA	Mummy??
AMMONIA	Corneous?
CORNEOUS	Mistress??

(*A beat.*)

LURCIO   You've met then.

                (AMMONIA *turns to* LURCIO.)

AMMONIA   What is going on here Lurcio? And why are
                you and Corneous wearing my clothes?

LURCIO   (*quickly*) We're drying them Mistress.
                We thought they would dry quicker if
                we walked around in them. (LURCIO *and*
                CORNEOUS *quickly walk up and down
                flapping their dresses to demonstrate their
                method.*)

AMMONIA   And what are you all doing?

                (LUDICRUS, SUSPENDA, NAUSIUS, VOLUPTUA,
                CORNEOUS *and* EROTICA *look totally
                non-plussed.* LURCIO *steps in with an
                explanation.*)

LURCIO   Well Mistress, your son Nausius was
                teaching his new friend Voluptua all about
                butterflies.

AMMONIA   Butterflies?

NAUSIUS   (*keenly*) I have written an ode.

LURCIO   I thought you might have. (NAUSIUS *hands
                him a scroll which* LURCIO *reads from.*) Let's
                have a look. "My love flies like a butterfly,
                upon a sea of ripples . . ." (*To audience.*)
                Wait for it, wait for it! (*Back to the scroll.*)
                "Her every wish is my command, as long as
                I see her . . . ears?"

NAUSIUS   I couldn't think of a rhyme there.

VOLUPTUA	I can!
LURCIO	Yes I bet you can!
AMMONIA	Such a sweet boy. Off you go then, Nausius. I'm sure you can find a way of entertaining your new friend.
NAUSIUS	Yes Mater. I'll do my best.
	(NAUSIUS *holds* VOLUPTUA'S *hand and they keenly exit into the bathroom.*)
AMMONIA	And what about you Erotica?
EROTICA	(*highly embarrassed*) Ah Mummy, yes well . . .
LURCIO	Your daughter was busy helping Corneous with his feet Mistress. You see they trouble him greatly and need constant massage.
AMMONIA	His feet?
LURCIO	Oh yes. His great big feet.
AMMONIA	I see.
	(EROTICA *and* CORNEOUS *heave a sigh of relief at* LURCIO'S *intervention.*)
LURCIO	It's sad but I'm afraid those feet of his will prevent any promotion around here.
AMMONIA	Yes, you're right. But he can still work with Cook in the kitchen. (*A triumphant* LURCIO *smiles at a defeated* CORNEOUS.) Meanwhile go and soak your feet in the house, Corneous.

CORNEOUS   Yes Mistress.

AMMONIA   And make sure he takes off my dress,
                Erotica.

EROTICA   (*keenly*) Leave it to me Mummy. I'll soon
                have it off!

                (EROTICA *and* CORNEOUS *exit into the house.*)

AMMONIA   And you Ludicrus? What are you doing with
                that awful woman again?

SUSPENDA   Who are you calling awful?

LUDICRUS   Well dear, now you see . . . the thing is . . .
                that Lurcio here . . .

AMMONIA   I thought I'd told you Lurcio that I didn't
                want her around here.

SUSPENDA   I am here you know.

LURCIO   Yes, well, she was just leaving when she . . .
                fainted!

SUSPENDA   Fainted??

LUDICRUS   Fainted. That's right. (*Sotto to* SUSPENDA.)
                Play along I beg you.

AMMONIA   Fainted? Again? What's the matter with the
                woman? She can't seem to go two minutes
                without collapsing.

LURCIO   You see once again the Master, out of the
                goodness of his heart, insisted on reviving
                her.

LUDICRUS   That's it. I was trying to stimulate her back
              to life.

SUSPENDA   I don't need any stimulation, believe me. All
              I remember is being invited to . . .

              (LURCIO *signals to* LUDICRUS *that he should
              pay* SUSPENDA *some money to buy her
              silence.* LUDICRUS *catches on and hands*
              SUSPENDA *some coins.*)

LUDICRUS   (*sotto to* SUSPENDA) My dear, here's a little
              something to help you with your memory.

              (SUSPENDA *stares at the money.*)

SUSPENDA   (*shocked*) What kind of a girl do you think I
              am?

LURCIO   (*sotto*) We all know what kind of a girl you
              are dear, we're just haggling over the price!

              (SUSPENDA *reacts.*)

AMMONIA   In my opinion what this woman needs is
              something hot inside her. (LUDICRUS *reacts.*)
              Take her into the kitchen Ludicrus and
              shove something in the oven.

LUDICRUS   Yes my dear. If you insist.

AMMONIA   I do.

              (*A relieved* LUDICRUS *grabs the bewildered*
              SUSPENDA *and leads her off into the house.*)

AMMONIA   Yes, well it's good to see that the household
              is running properly for once Lurcio. Just
              as well as I've got far too much on my
              mind at the moment. I'm off down to the

public baths. I'm hoping to meet an old
acquaintance. He won't get away from me
this time. Once he's clapped eyes on my
goggles – look out! (*She exits through the
gate.*)

(LURCIO *stands alone in the middle of the
courtyard. He turns and faces the audience.*)

LURCIO   (*to audience*) Phew! That was a close one,
didn't you think? But as usual yours truly
sorts it all out. Actually I think I was very
lucky don't you? The Mistress nearly found
out about everybody's shenanigans but
fortunately didn't. So we all get to lust for
another day. Well that lot do, I just get to
keep my job. Still I'm not complaining. At
least I didn't end up on a Mediterranean
cruise with no fun with that awful Captain
Treacherus.

(*Suddenly* TREACHERUS *is heard off.*)

TREACHERUS   (*off*) Will you leave me alone you revolting
man!!

LURCIO   Talking of which.

(*He quickly puts his wig back on. An out of
breath* TREACHERUS *runs on through the iron
gate.*)

TREACHERUS   Ammonia my dear! You must help me.

LURCIO   Oh? Are you having a hard time?

(*Whilst he talks,* TREACHERUS *hides behind a
pillar and keeps looking out for* KRETINUS.)

TREACHERUS   That buffoon Kretinus has gone berserk! He
              is like a sex maniac.

LURCIO   Shocking!

TREACHERUS   You're telling me.

LURCIO   (*inspired*) I could hide you.

TREACHERUS   Hide me?

LURCIO   Yes.

TREACHERUS   Yes?

LURCIO   In a little hidey-hole I know.

TREACHERUS   Hide me in a little hidey-hole you know?

LURCIO   Yes . . . is there an echo in here? (*To*
              TREACHERUS.) It's somewhere dark and
              private. Somewhere you'd be safe until I
              can join you.

TREACHERUS   But where Ammonia? Where?

LURCIO   In here. (*He unlocks the doors to the stable.*)

TREACHERUS   In the stable?

LURCIO   Bed down on the straw and as soon as I'm
              free I'll be along.

TREACHERUS   Oh my beautiful Ammonia. I won't forget
              this. (*He crosses to* LURCIO *and tries to kiss
              him.*)

LURCIO   (*pushing him away*) Yes, yes plenty of time
              for that later.

TREACHERUS   Of course my darling. (*He crosses to the stable doors.*)

LURCIO   And how about a little of this to make sure that my visit won't be a disappointment? (*He hands him a potion bottle.*)

TREACHERUS   Well I don't usually need any help.

LURCIO   Just to be sure.

TREACHERUS   Honestly, with my reputation it's not needed. Trust me.

LURCIO   Every little bit helps. (*He grabs* TREACHERUS'S *jowls and shakes them.*) Treacherus the lecherous!!

TREACHERUS   Oh very well. (*He takes a large swig from the bottle before exiting into the stable.*)

LURCIO   That's right. Go and warm up the shed. (*To the audience.*) Oh don't worry. I haven't given him the love potion. I'm not daft. I've given him the sleeping draught.

              (KRETINUS *runs on through the iron gate. He is wildly searching for* TREACHERUS.)

LURCIO   Part one of my plan is in place, now for part two.

KRETINUS   Where is he?

LURCIO   Where is who?

KRETINUS   Captain Treacherus. He's playing hard to get.

LURCIO   Is he?

KRETINUS   Yes but he knows I'm going to catch up with
                him. And then the orgy can commence!

LURCIO   Right.

KRETINUS   You're invited of course.

LURCIO   Of course, wouldn't miss it for the world.
                Got nothing on.

KRETINUS   That's the idea. So where is he?

LURCIO   He's hiding.

KRETINUS   Hiding?

LURCIO   In a hidey-hole.

KRETINUS   Where?

                (LURCIO *opens the stable doors and*
                KRETINUS *runs in rubbing his hands*
                together.)

KRETINUS   (*as he goes*) I won't forget this.

LURCIO   I'm sure you won't. Should be quite a party!
                (*To the audience.*) Job done. (*He locks the*
                stable doors and goes over to the well and
                drops the key into it. It hits the ground with
                a weak tinkle. As he had expected to hear a
                splash sound effect, LURCIO *makes the noise*
                himself.)

LURCIO   Splash! (*He scowls into the wings.*) Yes,
                cheers mate!! Thanks for nothing. (*To*
                audience.) Well there we are. Everything
                hunky-dory and neatly put to bed so to
                speak. That idiot Kretinus will be giving
                all his attention to that dreadful Captain

Treacherus who, by now, is probably fast
asleep. I think it will go down in the record
books as the first orgy for one!

Anyway it just remains for me to say
goodbye and to thank you all for dropping
in. Oh, before I go . . .

(*Suddenly there is a loud volcanic roar
off stage. An irritated* LURCIO *looks
disapprovingly into the wings.*)

Not yet! You're early. (*To audience.*) You
see the director wanted a big finish. I said
surely I could end on a high note and throw
a few funnies in. But oh no, that wasn't
good enough. Not for him, he's a stickler
for the old theatrics. He said it's Pompeii so
we'll have the volcano going off. You know
Vesuvius, a huge eruption and all the rest.
Lava and stuff! (*Another loud roar off.*) Not
yet, not yet! Honestly these stage hands –
they're too keen. Far too keen. Especially
that one, Tarquin. He's been trying it out
all afternoon, you know a sort of rehearsal.
The boy just can't keep his hands off the
knobs . . .

(*There is an enormous roar, A shaking*
LURCIO *grabs a pillar for support.* AMMONIA
enters through the iron gate.)

AMMONIA   (*screams*) Lurcio!! They've closed the
baths. They think it's the big one!!

(*Another huge roar.* AMMONIA *clings to a
pillar. There is much shaking and wobbling.
Smoke can be seen. The eruption causes
part of the scenery to fall down revealing
a half-naked* NAUSIUS *and* VOLUPTUA *in the*

*bathroom. They are not happy at being
discovered.* AMMONIA *is horrified.*)

AMMONIA   Nausius! What on earth!!!

LURCIO   Oh dear. Looks like things were on the up.
                 Still I'm sure he'll get an ode out of it.

                 (*Vesuvius roars again and another piece of
                 scenery falls away revealing* CORNEOUS *in a
                 romantic clinch with* EROTICA. *They look at
                 the audience highly embarrassed at being
                 discovered.*)

AMMONIA   Erotica!!

LURCIO   Better get those boots on and start walking,
                 Corneous.

                 (*More volcanic eruption and another
                 section of scenery falls to reveal a half-
                 naked* LUDICRUS SEXTUS *and* SUSPENDA. *He is
                 horrified at being caught.*)

AMMONIA   Ludicrus!!!

LURCIO   I suppose she's fainted again.

                 (*The whole set is now shaking. The doors
                 of the stable fall off their hinges and* SENNA
                 *appears pulling the cart behind her. On it
                 sit* TREACHERUS *and* KRETINUS. *They are both
                 tied up with their hands behind their backs
                 and are only wearing their underpants.*
                 TREACHERUS *is fighting the effects of the
                 sleeping potion.*)

TREACHERUS   (*heavily slurred*) Where are we going,
                 Kretinus? Some orgy?

SENNA   Back to my place!

KRETINUS   (*terrified*) No, no and thrice no!!

SENNA   (*keenly*) You mean go, go and thrice go?

KRETINUS   No, I mean nay, nay and thrice nay!!

                 (SENNA *cackles and the three of them exit
                 out through the iron gate.*)

LURCIO   More like lay, lay and thrice lay!! I bet she
                 didn't see that one coming.

                 (AMMONIA *is appalled by what she sees. She
                 turns on* LURCIO.)

AMMONIA   (*furious*) Lurcio!!!

NAUSIUS   Lurcio? Help!

EROTICA   Lurcio? Say something!

LUDICRUS   Lurcio? Do something! If you don't, it's the
                 . . . lions!

                 (*A beat.*)

LURCIO   Why is it always up to me? To be absolutely
                 frank it's your problem! I'm off. (*To
                 audience.*) I will leave you by quoting the
                 famous last words of Cleopatra to Mark
                 Antony – "If you've enjoyed it, tell your
                 friends!" Up Pompeii! Salute!!

                 (LURCIO *gives us his traditional two fingered
                 salute and then walks out through the iron
                 gate leaving everybody arguing with each
                 other.*

*Vesuvius erupts with the big one and
the stage goes white as falling ash rains
down through the smoke. The curtain falls
quickly.*)